SO, YOU WANT TO BE A PHYSICIAN?

Getting an Edge in your
Pursuit of the Challenging
Dream of Becoming a
Medical Professional

EDWARD M. GOLDBERG

ISBN-10: 1482684462
ISBN-13: 9781482684469

Library of Congress Control Number: 2013904647
CreateSpace Independent Publishing Platform North Charleston, SC

CONTENTS

ACKNOWLEDGMENTS

*First and foremost, I would like to thank my wife, Linda
Trytek, for her continuous love and support in spite of very
long work hours and the challenges of living with me.*

*I would also like to thank Elvira Krug, my assistant, for typing and
re-typing this book, and enduring the challenges of working with me.
My thanks also go to Angela Houghton, my research assistant, who
has been invaluable in helping organize the book, follow up on
student stories, and coordinate the placement of the book with an
editor and publisher. I appreciate the assistance of my high school
friend, Frank Shuftan, for serving as an initial editor of this book.*

*Finally, I would like to recognize all the students with whom I have
worked, some of whose academic brilliance and research achievements
have been exceptional. I look forward to great things from them.*

PROLOGUE

I have been a hospital administrator for thirty-eight years, and unlike many other hospital administrators, I've been known for being "physician-friendly." In that time, I have made close connections with thousands of physicians representing all subspecialties. Each day, I have been acutely aware of the joys and tribulations physicians encounter in practicing medicine.

I went to Northern Illinois University, where I received a Bachelor of Science in marketing and graduated cum laude. Then I received a Master of Science in hospital and health services administration from The Ohio State University.

So how did I come to write a book on how to get into medical school?

Approximately nine years ago, a member of my medical staff informed me that I had to get his son into medical school – or else. I explained to the physician that I had never really taken a full science course my entire life. I literally had to walk out of high school biology my first day because I couldn't stand to see the pinned, dead, stinking frogs, and the smell of formaldehyde made me want to vomit. I made an agreement with the teacher that I would write a paper on mitosis and meiosis rather than attend the lab. I lasted only one day in high school chemistry: when on the first day of the school year, the teacher gave us homework, I said, "That's it for me – you're not supposed to give homework the first day of class."

So how could I possibly help an individual get into medical school? The doctor's response was, "You're a smart guy – you'll figure it out."

I asked our hospital's legal counsel if this would be an acceptable service to perform from a Safe Harbor/Stark II perspective, and she indicated that if I offered the service to all employees and physicians, I could offer my tutoring services without legal risk. Safe Harbor/Stark II laws prohibit the provision of payment in cash or gifts in kind to induce a physician or other healthcare provider to refer patients to a hospital or other healthcare provider.

I have not only provided these services to children of employees and to members of the medical staff, but also to individuals who have called me up and stated they know "so-and-so," or are friends with "so-and-so," or heard that I can perform this service. I have never turned anybody down, and until writing this book, I never charged for the service. I asked only that they write to me after their interview and inform me if my coaching helped or not, and then provide me with the questions they were asked so that I could pass them on to others. I utilized this input, and my coaching experiences, to write this book and as the foundation for my coaching services.

My first student was just starting his sophomore year in college and attended an undergraduate program that had an affiliation with a medical school that would enroll two students each year in a guaranteed medical school program. This was a unique program that meant neither I nor he would have to worry about his MCAT scores. Given that I couldn't change his grade point average or activities, all I could really have an impact on was his personal statement and his interview abilities. He had good grades, was an Eagle Scout, and had done community service – and had gone on a mission trip to Peru – so I had a lot to work with.

I thought of several possible interview questions, which I still utilize today. The individual was successful, and seven years later I helped him prepare for an interview for an ENT residency position, which he received. I have since tutored scores of individuals, not only for traditional medical school programs, but six-to-eight-year medical school programs, dental school, veterinary school, residencies, physician assistant programs, and nurse practitioner programs. I have an impressive success rate. I recognize that many of the individuals who have come to me have had good grade point averages and good or great MCAT scores. Many have had solid activities, research, or service, but all my students have confirmed that I made a significant positive impact on their personal statements and their interview abilities.

It's ironic that an individual who never took science courses is teaching people to prepare for being a physician, dentist, veterinarian, physician assistant, or nurse practitioner, although I have had significant exposure to physicians in thirty-eight years as a hands-on, physician/employee-friendly hospital administrator.

What began as a service and an interesting hobby has evolved into this book, and a passionate new profession.

Finally, it's important to point out that the observations that follow throughout this book – such as the differences between male and female candidates – are based purely on my personal experiences and are not meant to reflect universal statements.

CHAPTER 1

WHY WOULD ANYONE WANT TO BE A PHYSICIAN?

I talk to numerous physicians every day. Many have told me that they are frustrated with medicine and have told their children not to try to become a physician. There is no question that these are very difficult times for physicians. They are being told what to do by the government, they are being told what to do by insurance and managed care companies, and they are being told what to do by hospitals. Physicians are increasingly losing their independence, which is one of the major reasons why individuals choose to become physicians. They are not only competing with other physicians, but with physician assistants and nurse practitioners in drug and grocery stores, and with hospitals. Reimbursements are declining, and physicians experience the same increasing pressures on their costs (i.e. malpractice insurance, technology, and hiring and maintaining employees) that all businesses encounter.

I often say, when the food on the table shrinks, table manners deteriorate. Right now, in healthcare, the food on the table is shrinking and table manners are deteriorating. Unfortunately, things are likely to become worse.

Although I often bemoaned the trials and tribulations that affected me as a hospital administrator, I would probably rather be a hospital administrator than a pediatrician who is paged almost every night he is on call to primarily respond to children's earaches. Or an obstetrician who might have to risk a malpractice lawsuit on every case he performs. Obstetricians might have to remain in the hospital for up to thirty-six hours for a delivery, which will then only pay $900. That fee usually includes the eight to twelve prenatal visits as well. With some malpractice carriers not wanting to insure physicians who have had three or more claims in the last ten years, even if the physician was found innocent, it's a career with challenges and stress on top of having someone's life in their hands.

On the other hand, there are many medical and surgical specialties where individual physicians can make an extremely handsome living, enjoy the respect and admiration of their patients and community, and remain very happy with their careers. Physicians do have the choice of becoming an employee of a hospital, or of a larger physician group, without having to be distracted by the tasks of operating a business. There would be no need to be concerned with hiring staff, performing billing functions, or enrolling in insurance and managed care plans. Alternatively, physicians still have the opportunity to run their own practice and be independent. There is also the satisfaction of helping people when they are most vulnerable.

Interestingly, most nurse practitioners, physician assistants, and certified nurses that I have talked with are generally very happy with their career choice.

CHAPTER 2

WHEN SHOULD YOU START THINKING ABOUT BECOMING A PHYSICIAN?

I often tell students that it is never too early to think about becoming a physician. By giving this career consideration early on, you can shape your academic classes and experiences to help you achieve your goal.

Many of the students who come to me have known they wanted to be a physician since elementary school.

This can affect the courses you take. For example, take as many science classes as possible. Advanced Placement science classes are even better. Also helpful as you pursue this goal is providing service in the healthcare world, perhaps by volunteering for a medical mission, or being a scribe in the ER.

But the gold standard is working in a research lab – even if it's doing what may appear to be a menial task. If the opportunity presents itself, don't miss out, and if the opportunity doesn't present itself, seek out that opportunity.

CHAPTER 3

THINK OF GETTING INTO MEDICAL SCHOOL LIKE STAYING IN A HOTEL

There are 159 medical schools in the United States (133 M.D. and 26 D.O.), 54 in Mexico, and 59 in the Caribbean.

For the United States in 2006, there were 39,108 medical school applicants, and 21,000 were *not* accepted. In 2011 there were 43,919 applications.

Applicants for medical school average 28 points of a possible 45 on the MCAT. Individuals who ultimately become medical school students average 32 points. The grade point average of accepted students is 3.5 to 3.8.[1]

I have seen an increase in students who had either a low grade point of between 3.2 and 3.5, or a low MCAT score of between 26 and 29. They felt they could compensate for this by having a whole list of extracurricular activities – shadowing physicians, working in clinics, being an EMT, being involved in various sports (sometimes as team captain) and religious activities, playing musical instruments, and so on.

I don't want to break the students' hearts or their spirits, but I tell them that medical school could be considered like a hotel. The most important thing about a hotel is that it be clean and that there be a bed and clean sheets. You might go to the Ritz Carlton, and they might have terrycloth slippers and a bathrobe and chocolates, but if there is no bed, they don't meet the essence of being a hotel. I explain to students that if they took all the time they spent on their extracurricular activities and channeled that time into either studying to get better grades or taking a Kaplan course or individual tutoring for a better MCAT score, they would be much better off.

---

[1] Association of American Medical Colleges

Remember, the two main components of getting into a medical school are your grades and your MCAT score. Without them you don't get to talk with me about improving your personal statement and interview abilities. Yes, some service is good because it shows that you want to help others. Perhaps one other activity is appropriate to show that you are a multidimensional person. Research is always a plus because it demonstrates an intellectual pursuit and the desire to learn. However, a two-, three-, or four-page listing of extracurricular activities does not help if your grades and MCAT scores are below par. My suggestion is to concentrate on your grades and the MCAT, which will get you the interview, and then work on providing the best personal statement and interview possible.

SO, YOU WANT TO BE A PHYSICIAN?

CHAPTER 4

HOW TO PREPARE FOR BECOMING A PHYSICIAN

My advice is to get the highest grades you possibly can, particularly in science. Media articles cited in this book suggest that in 2015, the updated MCAT will require students to have a firm understanding of biochemistry, molecular biology, statistics, psychology, and sociology.[2] Also, score as high as you can on either the ACT if you are going to apply for a six-to-eight-year medical school program, or the MCAT if you will have an undergraduate degree in biology or chemistry. If you are offered the opportunity to take an anatomy course, take it.

I have found an uncanny direct relationship between the ACT score and the MCAT score. Typically, whatever the percentage ranking a student receives in the ACT, he or she receives a similar percentage ranking in the MCAT.

I highly recommend that students take the Kaplan or other formal course for both the ACT and the MCAT. I also strongly encourage individual tutoring in addition to the Kaplan courses. I have found that the Kaplan course usually increases the score in both the ACT and the MCAT by 1 to 2 points, and I have seen similar improvement via individual tutoring. Two to four points can easily make the difference in being accepted or not. Although the majority of the students I have talked to said, "Oh, I read a guidebook on my own," I recommend more formal guidance, as indicated above.

Additionally, for those who want to go to college and not a six-to-eight-year medical school program, my advice is to get into the best school you can. I know one physician, now a well-regarded subspecialist, who went to a well-respected university for his undergraduate

---

[2] "Future pre-meds will take new MCAT" by Traci Tillman, Yale Daily News, April 6, 2011

program and only achieved a 3.4 grade point average. Even with a respectable score of 29 on the MCAT, he ended up going to a Caribbean medical school. He felt going to a higher quality undergraduate program actually hurt him.

It's hard to judge, and it can be the luck of the draw, i.e., who knows what teachers and what classes an individual participates in. However, at the end of the day, a higher grade point average from a less prestigious school would probably trump a lower grade point average from a better school, within reason, i.e., a delta of at least 0.3 or 0.4. Obviously, the best scenario is to have a great grade point average from a great school, so I'll stick with my original advice. Go to the best school you can get into, get the highest grade point average you can, and try for an even higher average in the sciences than your overall grade point average.

CHAPTER 5
SIX-TO-EIGHT-YEAR MEDICAL SCHOOL PROGRAMS

Approximately 15 percent of the students who I have coached have applied for six-to-eight-year medical school programs. Some parents of students feel that the students might not be mature enough for a six-to-eight-year program, but my general feeling is that a bird in the hand is worth two in the bush. If an individual can be accepted to a six-to-eight-year medical school program, take it.

However, all of the six-to-eight-year programs that I am aware of have a minimum grade point average that must be maintained or you risk being disenrolled from the program. You may still go to that college, but you will no longer be in the six-to-eight-year guaranteed program. In some schools, the expected grade point average can be as low as 3.5, but it is typically a 3.65 or 3.75.

I worked with one student who did not maintain the required average and was dropped from the program. The student still had the opportunity to make a recovery by getting good grades and taking the MCAT for medical school, but for me it's kind of like the Woody Allen movie *Annie Hall*, where he suggested they kiss at the beginning of the date so they could get the tension over with. I feel the same way about the six-to-eight-year programs. If you can get in – why not?

SO, YOU
WANT TO BE
A PHYSICIAN?

CHAPTER 6

BEST PRE-MEDICAL SCHOOL ACTIVITIES

Although most parents feel that volunteering in a hospital is a meaningful experience, and will help their children get into medical school, I don't believe that this is valid anymore.

I believe the new gold standard for activities that will help applicants get into medical school is, first and foremost, research. Even if it's minimal, this experience can be impressive, particularly if the student is asked back for a second or third year by a professor or physician who is leading the research. If the student can articulate the research, it's a plus in both the personal statement and the interview. If the student can articulate the research passionately, it's a bigger plus.

Secondly, a medical mission trip is always helpful because it's not only impressive in the student's personal statement, but can be utilized in interviews. Medical mission trips demonstrate that the student has a passion for helping others. I have never had a medical student encounter a problem by mentioning participation in a medical mission during an interview. During a medical mission, students perform functions that are appropriate (taking a history and physical, teaching patients about hygiene, taking weights and heights, etc.), and every student I have coached has indicated that this assisted them in their interview process.

There was one student whose father was an oral surgeon, who came to me one year after he was not accepted to dental school. In the student's first interview with me, the student told me he informed the interviewer that he personally performed extractions during a medical mission in Africa. I felt the student was trying to impress the dentist conducting the interview, but American Dental Association bylaws indicated that no one should perform any function for which they were not licensed in America – even if they were in Africa. The student was turned down.

Although I continue to believe that medical missions are important, I always advise students that they shouldn't do anything that they are not licensed to perform in America.

The third most helpful experience is that of a scribe in the emergency department of a hospital. This is a relatively new field. Typically, these individuals are college graduates who are in the emergency room transcribing the physicians' orders. They get to see a wide range of medical and surgical experiences, and can utilize this as an excellent knowledge base in the personal statement and during the interview process.

CHAPTER 7

THE PERSONAL STATEMENT

As I've mentioned, great grades, meaningful activities, and nailing the tests get your foot not only on the ladder, but can put you a few steps up on the competition. But that's mostly the quantitative side of things.

Now it's time to show quality in two areas of critical importance: the personal statement and the interview process. Here is where the careful reader, and serious medical school candidate, will find value added.

I have advised my students and their parents repeatedly that they should show me their personal statement well before they turn it in so that I can make suggestions or possible revisions. Unfortunately, a high percentage of students send me their personal statements after they already sent it in to their schools of choice, or they send it to me the day before it is due. I usually respond, "What do you expect me to do? We can't change it because it's already been sent in." Or, I try to expedite a one-day exchange of suggestions. Some students and their parents will call me the day before their interview, even after I have explained and stressed repeatedly that it is a multi-week process.

I believe the personal statement usually needs to tell a story in a very distinct fashion. Many schools might say, "Describe a challenge that has changed your life," or "Describe a challenge that you have overcome." I have found that many students have something they want to include in their statement, often experiences or activities they are proud of; for example, an individual applying to dental school stated she was the president of the Pre-Med Club. I advised her not to include that in her personal statement because it would look to the dental school as if they were second fiddle. But, no, the student spent time doing it, she was proud of it, and by goodness she was going to put it in there.

So, the most important thing is that the student carefully reviews what it is the schools are asking – and then respond to what they're asking, rather than what the student might want to say. I know this can be hard.

Assuming that the personal statement allows you to say whatever you want and does not have specific instructions, the student can choose to highlight good grades, MCAT score, research experience, mission trip, or healthcare experience. I prefer to stick to a pretty normal path, starting with an interest and achievement in the sciences, and then discussing overall grades if they are positive. If the science grades are better than the overall grades, mention it. If not, do not lie; simply mention what your science grade point average is. If your overall GPA is better than your science GPA, which would be unfortunate, simply stress your overall GPA.

Typically, I like to see some type of unique experience, such as valedictorian, salutatorian, Eagle Scout, leader in a group, research assistant, or any meaningful project or mission to help the community or humanity. Finally, the student should demonstrate commitment to helping others. If you have the grades and the ACT or MCAT, and some unique personal service or mission, I would go with that.

Many students think they need to be cute or unique, or think that they need to differentiate themselves by providing responses that are too extreme. If you don't have an ideal GPA or MCAT score, then you may need to explain the deficiency. Perhaps there is a legitimate explanation, which would be great, but be careful. Explanations that may involve drinking before the test, ADD, or breaking up with your boyfriend could just get you in more trouble. However, unfortunate legitimate explanations such as contracting mono or having a family member die, could help explain a deficiency appropriately. But if you have demonstrable excellence in these areas, I recommend sticking to the basics.

SO, YOU WANT TO BE A PHYSICIAN?

CHAPTER 8

THE INTERVIEW PROCESS,
i.e., The Goldberg Method

First, I'm like a psychiatrist or a journalist interviewing the student and trying to pull out every bit of information the student has – grades, coursework, ACT, MCAT scores, community service, volunteering, mission trip, Boy Scouts, Girl Scouts, research, sports, hobbies, and interests. Everything, including the kitchen sink.

If Art Linkletter were still alive, I could send him some of the things my students have said to me in the very first session that would surpass the statements made by kids from the show *Kids Say the Darnedest Things*. I could also send them to Ripley, but he wouldn't believe it.

Now, I understand that because it's a very informal discussion and I'm not "threatening," students may say things to me that they might not say in front of a physician from a medical school admissions committee. Although most statements are appropriate, I have had students tell me the following reasons when I first ask them why they want to be a physician:

- "I think it would be great to get girls."
- "I think it would be a lot of fun."
- "My mom wants me to be a physician."
- "My dad wants me to be a physician."
- "My grandfather wants me to be a physician."
- "I could make a lot of money."
- "I think it would be the right profession for me."
- And the all-too-familiar, "I want to help people."

I wish I were joking, but I'm not. It's at this stage in the game that I explain to the students that their desired medical school was not founded in 1859 so that 150 years later they could have fun or make a lot of money by being a physician. I explain that they have to sell themselves to the school and explain what they can contribute to the school, the other students, humanity, and the field of medicine.

Then I become a playwright. The student writes the script, and I make recommendations. Our goal is to provide distinct responses to at least three and possibly four questions, each of which should be no more than one paragraph, and each of which needs to be memorized exactly as we write them.

We therefore use a conversational, not formal, writing style. The student will write responses to at least the following three questions:

1. Tell me about yourself.
2. Why do you want to be a physician?
3. Why do you want to go to XYZ medical school?

I believe that in most business interviews, the interviewer asks himself if the interviewee is someone he would want to work with. I believe that internally this decision is made very rapidly. I think it's the same for medical school interviews. That's the reason I place so much emphasis on really getting down the answers to three questions instead of hundreds of questions. I believe one of these questions is usually asked at the beginning of the interview, and once the tone is set in a positive fashion, I think the game is usually won.

What I really want the students to do is have the individual who is interviewing them end up rooting for them. I can see it in my own interactions with the students who come to me. The ones I am rooting for are the ones for whom I will give extra-special effort, because I really want them to be accepted. It's an unbelievable feeling when they call me, even before they call their parents, to tell me that the interview went well, or later, that they were accepted to medical school. The bottom line: *the purpose of all interviews is for the interviewees to have the interviewers root for them.*

The first two responses, i.e., to the questions "Tell me about yourself" and "Why do you want to be a physician?" can be drawn from the information provided in the initial practice interview.

The response to the third question, "Why this medical school?" needs to be researched specifi-cally to match that medical school. In other words, the student needs to go online and find out what is unique about the medical school of interest, and then follow up with the school after the interview, if possible. Some medical schools provide clinical experience in the first year; others make you wait. Professor/student ratio, what types of programs and research are performed, and other information should be reviewed so that students can sufficiently articulate why they want to go to this particular medical school. If students know someone in that medical school, they should seek him or her out and ask questions so they can reference this feedback (hopefully positive) in the interview.

Typically students will draft their responses, and because I interviewed them and know their total inventory of assets and attributes, I am able to guide them and ask why they left something out or put something in. Typically they e-mail this to me and I make suggestions, possibly additions or deletions, and we repeat the process until both the student and I are happy with the finished product.

There are occasions in which the student and I do not agree, and I tell them it's their life and not mine, and I always defer to their judgment. But I try to explain to them why they should or shouldn't include a specific item.

After we reach agreement – or not – the students take the final product, whatever it is, and memorize it. Not only memorize it, but "be it." Like Chevy Chase in the movie *Caddy Shack* when he said, "You have to be the ball." You need to be the script. I then provide some general comments, and then I move from being like a psychiatrist/journalist/screenwriter to a nun with a ruler going over and over the script.

One of my general rules is do not start a sentence with "well." For some reason, I have found this to occur almost ubiquitously among men and women of all cultures and nationalities.

The following are no-no's:

Well...
Ahh...
Uhh...
Umm...
Well, actually...
To tell the truth...
To be honest with you...

I explain to students that when they say, "Well actually...To be honest with you...To tell you the truth," that actually means that everything they've said before that was a lie.

While we are going through the interview process, I literally keep a scorecard of the above no-no's, and after the students finish each rehearsal, I tell them and show them how many times they said one until I hopefully "sensitize" the use of those words out of them.

After I believe they know the script *cold*, we work on the following:

1. **Smoothness.** Several of my students (mostly men) would look up in the air or shake their head as if they were reading the script in their mind. For these students I tell them that their responses need to come off naturally and smoothly, and if they bang their head or look up in the sky for the answer, it literally shows that they have memorized a script. Doing so blows the entire process.

2. **Eye contact.** I've learned an amazing thing from this process. Almost every female seems to provide good, natural eye contact, and almost universally, males do not. Men look down, look away, look over your head, or look up at the ceiling. I need to work on men with this problem and sometimes have to say, "I'm over here." Why this is I'm not sure, but I assume it's because women naturally seem to be concerned with others and most men just care about themselves.

3. **What do you do with your hands and feet?** Once again, most women seem to naturally know what to do with their hands. They keep them gently at their sides or in their lap but use them occasionally to make a point or show enthusiasm. Men, on the other hand, don't seem to be able to utilize their hands appropriately. Most of the time, the men's hands are like a robot, stiff and at their sides, not moving during our entire discussion. On a rare occasion, their hands are waving up and down and are all over the place. Similar to a woman's use of her hands, the man's hands should be quietly at his side or on his lap but utilized occasionally to stress a point or express passion. Legs should be relatively still, no shaking up and down, changing positions only infrequently.

4. **Posture.** Probably 60 percent of the individuals I teach are women and 40 percent are men. Almost every single female, irrespective of culture or ethnicity, has had good posture. They sit upright toward the middle front of the chair, leaning slightly toward the interviewer; their body language says they are interested. Men, on the other hand, typically lean back lazily as though they are in their bedroom talking to some friends, or they sit up stiff like a robot. I explain to them that this will be the most important interview of their life, and to demonstrate interest they need to sit toward the front middle of the chair, back erect, leaning slightly toward the person with whom they are talking. Sounds simple, but you would be amazed how difficult this can be for some men.

5. **How you dress.** Once again, the women seem for the most part to dress appropriately and on occasion come slightly overdressed. Almost every male student has come in messy: 95 percent in gym shoes, 5 percent in flip-flops, typically wearing a shirt without a collar, and often with messy hair.

   The only problem I have found with women is that approximately 20 percent have a nervous, inappropriate giggle or laugh. Unlike the men, where training has to be constant and hard, all I need to say to most women one time is, "Oh, so you're going to be a physician and tell Mrs. Jones her husband died and then giggle." After that, they typically take the criticism constructively, and the giggle does not occur again. Why women seem to be able to utilize feedback appropriately, but similar advice proves to be more difficult for men, I really don't understand. My wife says that culturally women are trained to respond to expectations and criticism more than men, and that women, as child bearers, are hard-wired to use eye contact to gain nonverbal information from others. I have no idea why, but there is a huge difference in interviewing ability between men and women.

6. **Practice, practice, practice.** I tell the students it's important to practice, not only alone, sometimes in the mirror, but with someone else to look at the script and go through it with them.

   My philosophy is that although there are likely to be numerous questions asked during an interview, I encourage students to focus on just three main potential questions. Preparing for one or two more questions based on unique circumstances can also be appropriate. One of those questions might be "Why did you wait one year after college to apply to medical school?"

7. **The elephant in the room.** If there is an obvious shortcoming or deficiency in your body of work – e.g., you had a very poor GPA your first year but later made a recovery, or you had great grades and great research, but blew the MCAT – I believe it is important to mention the elephant in the room. They've seen your scores and transcript, they know it, and they are probably too polite to ask about it, so you might as well address it. If there is a unique circumstance that's explainable, I say throw the Hail Mary and explain it.

   I believe one of my most gratifying and meaningful coaching achievements involved a student who was a wonderful individual, attended a decent medical school, had a class rank near the middle of the pack, and had National Board scores of approximately 50 percent. This student really wanted to be a dermatologist. The student applied for the first residency match and did not match. Although she could have received an internal medicine residency at a very decent program, she wanted to be a dermatologist – or not be a physician at all. I hadn't counseled this student yet, but knew her father and saw them at our annual holiday party, and I offered my assistance. The student refused to accept my assistance. I tried to talk the student out of being a dermatologist, indicating that it is typically the top 1 percent of the class and 1 percent in the National Boards that are accepted to a dermatology residency, but this individual was determined to be a dermatologist.

After medical school this individual worked, without payment, for one year with a dermatologist who had an affiliation with a medical school. The individual assisted in writing an article for a dermatology journal, and continued on to apply again for a dermatology residency. Again, no match.

The next year, this individual continued to refuse my offer of assistance. She worked on another article and a chapter of a dermatology book with a different person loosely affiliated with a teaching program. The individual then applied again for a dermatology residency and still did not match.

Now, the individual came to me and asked for assistance. In my long interview with the student, I asked if any of the interviewers asked about class rank or National Board scores. The individual indicated that the interviewers did not ask about either. I explained that, in my opinion, there was a bubble over the individual's head that the professors were looking at rather than at the student. The bubble said, "I only received 50 percent in the National Boards and 50 percent in the class ranking." Why would they pick anyone who had those statistics when they could have individuals in the top 1 percent of each? I indicated that I felt the interviewee needed to address the elephant in the room, and if the professors didn't bring it up, she would need to. The goal was to draw the attention of the interviewers to the person, her passion and achievements, and not her National Board scores.

When I asked the student why she wanted to be a dermatologist, she indicated that it was because dermatology made her feel like a well-rounded and total physician – finding the problem through observation, confirming it through pathology, and taking an action to correct it via surgery or medication. I have talked to many medical students who wanted to be dermatologists, and I felt that many of them wanted to be dermatologists because they were students who always wanted and achieved the best. They went to the best colleges, were first in their class, and went to the best medical schools because they were the best, and they wanted to be dermatologists because they were told that's the best specialty to be in. I knew other medical students who wanted to be dermatologists because of the high pay. Others desired the lifestyle, and some didn't want to be burdened by a pager, which almost all other specialties require.

This individual wanted to be a dermatologist because it made her feel like a total physician. The student had a passion and unquenchable desire. I suggested that she utilize the phrase "National Board scores don't take care of patients – physicians do." Then the interviewee could go on to explain that many individuals want to be dermatologists for the reasons mentioned above, but this individual wanted to be a dermatologist because of her passion for the specialty. The student had already proven her passion through the articles and chapter that she had contributed, and through her continuing efforts and determination to persevere in the specialty.

When I received a call from this student saying that she felt this final interview had gone much better than the prior ones, I started to cry, as I was really rooting for this individual to succeed. I felt she really deserved it. I would go to this person if she became a dermatologist. It was with equal tears when the individual called to tell me that she had been accepted in a dermatology residency. I thought, good for this student and good for the program that was smart enough to see the true qualities of this physician above her Board scores.

I had another individual who had a mediocre GPA at a mediocre college and a mediocre MCAT score. During my questioning, I spent over an hour with this individual trying to find if he had done anything unique. I repeatedly asked if he had done any research. To add to my disappointment, I felt the individual was generally unenthusiastic. I actually told the student I didn't think I could help him as there was no hook, like being an Eagle Scout or going on a medical mission. So after I told the individual that I didn't think there was anything I could do and I was walking him to the door, I asked again, for what was now the fourth time, if there was anything unique or special in his background that could be utilized during an interview. Did he receive any awards, complete any research, or have a particular passion? Finally, he indicated that he had been working in a lab in southern Illinois on the weekends for the past two years.

I told the individual to have a seat again and tell me about what he did in the lab. He told me about his experience at the lab with an illumination, brightness, and enthusiasm that he hadn't displayed in the previous hour. He intricately explained his work placing probes on mice and performing EEGs under different scenarios. It sounded to me like exciting, meaningful research, and the individual sounded excited and enthusiastic about it. I said, "Don't change one word, and describe this in your interview exactly as you just did to me with the same level of enthusiasm." I indicated that even if the interviewer introduced himself and then ended the interview that, no matter what, his description of the research needed to be told to his interviewers. This individual was accepted into medical school.

8. If they ask you if you have any questions, you should be prepared to ask something. Two possible suggestions are:

    a. What made you want to become part of the faculty here?
    b. What about this program are you most proud of?

GREAT ANSWERS TO THE "THREE QUESTIONS"

1. Tell me about yourself

- I graduated from Boston University with a BA in psychology and biology. Throughout my life I have had passions for understanding the complex human body and helping those in need. Growing up in New York City with Spanish physicians as parents, I developed a great appreciation for the customs and traditions of different cultures. I speak both Spanish and English, and I became deeply fascinated with the human body. I consider myself a very social person, and I love to talk and interact with people. My love for interacting and my passions have led me to volunteer throughout my life, travel to Honduras on a global medical brigade, and tutor inner city Chicago public high school students. Although I struggled freshman year in college, my perseverance and optimistic attitude allowed me to adapt new learning strategies to ultimately succeed.

- I am from Algonquin IL, attended Jacobs High School, and graduated with a 3.9 GPA. While I was there, I was involved with the music program. I played the violin and even had the opportunity to be section leader and first chair of my high school orchestra. I was also an executive board member in the music honor society, Tri-M, and acted in just about every play and musical offered at my high school. I was also very involved with the National Honor Society and performed service projects in the community and worked with every age, from elementary school to people in the nursing homes.

- I've wanted to be a dentist from a young age and have interned with Dr. S. and Dr. D. to further my interest in the dental field. Along with my studies, I have been involved in my service fraternity, Alpha Phi Omega. I've caroled for nursing homes, painted at a women's shelter, and volunteered at carnivals for kids with special needs. I am also a morale captain for Dance Marathon. In that position, I make trips to the University of Iowa Children's Hospital and encourage people to help raise money for the Dance Marathon event. I am an active member of the art group called Artisans, which allows me to experience different forms of art. I've worked with fine art, glass, jewelry, paints, and even pottery. I am currently a senior attending Augustana College and am finishing my biology major and biochemistry minor.

During my time at college I have had the opportunity to have different research experiences with two different professors: Dr. G. on the topic of hominid tooth evolution and Dr. S. on the topic of oral microorganisms. These were both interesting topics, and I enjoyed having the opportunity to work one-on-one with these two professors. I also have three jobs on campus. I am a morning worker for the recreation center, an admissions ambassador that gives tours and calls prospective students, and an anatomy tutor.

- I attended Carl Sandburg High School, and my grade point average overall was 4.069 and my science average was 4.125. I was actively involved on the tennis team. I played second doubles and qualified for state all four years. My freshman and sophomore years, we finished sixth in state, and my junior and senior years, we finished fourth in state. I've also volunteered for four years at St. Alexius Medical Center in Hoffman Estates, and was asked to apply for a position in the Radiology Department. I have very much enjoyed my time here at St. Xavier, and my GPA is 3.95. I also am secretary of Kappa Kappa Gamma sorority and am still an active leader on the tennis team as I play the top spot for singles and doubles. I am also the public relations co-chairman of the pre-health club and a member of Habitat for Humanity.

- I grew up in Highland Park, IL, and went to Highland Park High School. My mom works for a non-profit art organization called Art Encounter, and my father is a physician. I graduated from the University of Pittsburgh in 2009 with a 3.5 GPA. My senior year I was active in research working for the Behavioral Medicine Research Group, where I trained participants to use devices that measure stress in real time. I'm an avid soccer player. I played all four years in high school and am still playing in leagues in the Chicagoland area. In addition to soccer, I enjoy cooking and reading. I also recently started playing golf again after adjusting my horrendous swing.

- I grew up in Arlington Heights IL, attended Buffalo Grove High School, and am now a senior at Duke University. I am a biology major with a chemistry minor and a certificate in global health. I have an overall GPA of 3.82 and a science GPA of 3.92, and I obtained a 38 overall score on the MCAT. I have developed a passion for global health throughout my time at Duke and pursued this passion by writing and being awarded a grant to conduct research on childhood under-nutrition in rural southwestern Kenya the summer before my junior year. I have ample leadership experience through the Duke organization Project WILD, where twice a year I have led crews of seven to ten inexperienced freshmen on a one- or two-week backpacking trip. This past summer I shadowed a pediatric infectious disease specialist at John Stroger Hospital once a week. Lastly, I have also been involved in various other organizations through Duke University, from tutoring elementary children to working in a *Drosophila* lab.

- I am from Palatine and come from a family of doctors. My parents are both internists. For high school I went to Loyola Academy in Wilmette. It was far from my house, but I could not have asked for a better high school experience. A unique aspect of my high school was the awesome service opportunities that were there. My favorite experience was traveling down to Cairo, IL, to fix up broken-down homes and stores. It was refreshing to see the citizens we worked with remain enthusiastic and optimistic despite living in a ravaged town.

  I attended college at Georgetown and looked to provide service with a medical focus. I became a part of the Georgetown Emergency Response Medical Services. As a biochemistry major, I wanted to learn how the scientific process is explored as part of a lab group. I joined Dr. T.'s analytical chemistry lab group to analyze molecular effects on fuel cells. I synthesized platinum polyoxometallae nanoparticles and analyzed their electrochemical properties to determine their stability and potential suitability for fuel cells. The American Chemical Society awarded me with the College Chemistry Achievement Award for my work inside and outside the classroom.

  When I was not working in the lab or as an EMT, I worked as the director of purchasing at an on-campus grocery store. I coordinated orders with more than forty vendors on a weekly basis and was able to introduce some new health-related products to the Georgetown community. I graduated from Georgetown this past May and have been working as an emergency room scribe for doctors.

- I was born and raised around Naperville, a suburb of Chicago. My mother is a pediatric anesthesiologist, and my father is a communications engineer. I am a senior at MIT, where I'm majoring in aerospace engineering with information technology and minoring in public policy. I am fundamentally a problem solver – I see a problem or a need, and I try to address it. From my Eagle project when I was a Boy Scout, to my engineering major and my work as an EMT, I have always tried to fix things. In addition to this, I have a wide variety of interests. I really like learning about politics and history; hence, my public policy minor. I also enjoy sailing, scuba diving, hiking, and many other activities, but fundamentally if I can make something better, if I see a need that I can address, if I see an improvement that can be made – I'll do it.

- I grew up in Buffalo Grove, IL, and I am the son and nephew of two pediatricians, so I have been exposed to pediatrics my whole life. I received my undergraduate education at the University of Rochester, where I played baseball, majored in chemistry, and minored in Spanish. I currently attend Rush Medical College in Chicago and finished in the top third of my class, and I received a 222 on USMLE Step 1 and a 248 on USMLE Step 2 CK. Besides academics during medical school, I am most proud of the work that I have done at NLVS, which is a clinic in West Rogers Park in Chicago. The clinic is entirely student-run and it serves primarily the South Asian community. I've volunteered there once or twice a quarter since my M1 year. I was also the Rush treasurer for a year and raised more than five hundred dollars by organizing a medical school basketball tournament. Besides medicine, I am obsessed with Chicago sports and have started running and biking. I recently completed two races called Muddy Buddies and the Urbanathlon. My ultimate goals are to finish a triathlon and a marathon.

- I am a triple major in biology, pre-medicine, and psychology at Augustana College, and I have always had interests in the sciences and in helping others. I intern for the Child Abuse Council and volunteer at a women's abuse shelter. I have learned the impact that one person can make, and similar to my experience on the crew team, I can see the impact that people working together can have. I have been blind in one eye since birth and am an asthmatic, which limited me athletically and socially as a child, so I devoted my childhood to learning and helping others. Above all, I want to be able to use my knowledge to help people.

2. Why do you want to be a physician?

- Growing up, family dinners were dominated by conversations regarding coagulation factors or the GI tract. My parents would quiz me days later, and I would strive to better understand what they were trying to teach me. Ever since, I developed an immense fascination for science, especially for the human body, and have always wanted to keep learning. Also, when my family moved to Oak Park, IL, from Barcelona, our community helped my family find good schools, learn American traditions and quickly make friends because my brother and I were lonely. These experiences instilled in me an unrelenting passion to give back to my community – just as my community helped me – and conduct research to better understand the beautifully complex human body.

- I've wanted to be a physician for as long as I can remember. In grammar school I loved science classes and participating in the science fairs. I remember all of my science fair projects, from paper machete volcanoes to potato clocks. My mother is a pharmacist, my father is a physician, and my older brother just completed medical school at Rush and will be entering an ENT residency in Gainesville. Between high school and college, my family took a service trip to Peru and helped the poor and needy, and it made a significant impression on me about the positive impact that one person can make. I have seen the positive impact my parents have on others as health care professionals and the great satisfaction that both of them receive in helping others. My desire to become a physician was heightened to an even greater extent when I volunteered at St. Alexius Medical Center. I am committed to being a physician and helping others.

- My first interest in the profession came after I injured my knee playing soccer in college. I was treated by Dr. B. and his PA, Travis. Travis saw me for most of my pre-operative and post-operative appointments. I was really impressed with Travis's care for me throughout my treatment, and I committed to learning more about the profession, as well as sports medicine. Although Travis piqued my interest in the profession, I was not absolutely sure the PA profession was right for me until after my shadowing experiences. I shadowed several PAs in orthopedics and dermatology, and they all said they felt their job was rewarding and stimulating. I liked how each PA I shadowed had a good rapport with the doctors, working well with them as part of a team, but also working autonomously – in some cases seeing patients the whole day without the doctor on staff. I am also interested in the profession because the PA degree is so diverse. One PA I shadowed practiced in an emergency room setting and was hired to work in orthopedics without having to retrain. Finally, I enjoy working with patients, and I liked the fact that the PAs I shadowed were able to spend a little more time with the patients than other healthcare members did.

- Medicine is at the intersection of everything I could want from a career. It involves working with people, lifelong learning, and the ability to help others. It also helps that I find the body, how it works, and how to manipulate it fascinating. My time in Kenya has made a huge impact on my life, and I have wanted to go back ever since I stepped onto the airplane in Nairobi. My dream is to spend time working with the underserved populations, such as those in Kenya, and (*insert medical school name*) will give me the skills and tools I need to bring about a real change. I am aware of the dedication needed during the minimum of seven years until I can finally be a physician, and I relish the challenge.

- The biological sciences have always fascinated me. In fifth grade I gave a report on a future career as a doctor, and I can vividly remember sharing my edible model of the eukaryotic cell with my seventh grade class. My experiences and education as an under-graduate have fostered an intrigue for the practical applications of my studies. Medicine is a challenging career path, but it will allow me to help others and contribute to the community. It is special because the physician has the opportunity to relate to patients on a personal level and profoundly influence their lives. My grandpa was a physician who loved his work and was clearly moved by his encounters in medicine. After retiring at seventy-five, he still attended medical conferences with my mother and tried to keep up with medical news. As I get older, I hope to maintain the passion for my work as my grandpa did for his. Medicine is a line of work where knowledge and procedural techniques are always changing. The dynamic atmosphere promises a job that will keep me on my toes while fulfilling a need to do something good for the community.

- I think medicine is a truly noble profession because of its focus on improving the lives of others. In addition, I think that being a doctor provides an opportunity for a varied and fulfilling professional life. A doctor can and sometimes must be a researcher, problem-solver, businessperson, and leader in addition to a clinician, and I plan on embracing all of these roles fully.

- I've known from a very young age that I wanted to be a dentist because I've always had a fascination with teeth. Before one of my parents would have a dental appointment, I would actually put on my mom's dishwashing gloves and look in my parent's mouth and check for cavities. When I reached the eighth grade, I attended a career fair where a dentist gave a presentation on his occupation. I just remember feeling so excited when I heard about the different tasks of a dentist, such as working with your hands on a fine level and using that ability to help people. In high school I decided to further my interest in dentistry by interning with Dr. S. I became familiar with the tools and procedures, and Dr. S. even let me observe him on a regular basis, which was very exciting. It was such a great experience because I not only saw different procedures, I also worked as a receptionist at his office. Along with the internship, I was very involved with orchestra and continued my hobbies in making jewelry and even being ambitious enough to make dollhouses. By playing the violin and working with art, I noticed my dexterity and attention to fine detail improved. Along with handwork, I have always loved helping people, so I decided to join the National Honor Society. I was a dedicated member and really enjoyed working in underserved areas. While attending college I had the opportunity to focus my interest on teeth through research with some of my college professors. My sophomore year I worked with Professor G. on the topic of hominid tooth evolution. Together we studied the structure of teeth to understand the evolutionary transition of the hominid species, and our research found that *Australopithecus africanus* is the closest genus to *Homo sapiens*. My passion to help others led me to a service fraternity called Alpha Phi Omega. In that group I plan activities to reach out to the needy. I have arranged caroling events and a senior citizen prom at a nursing home, and I've even made hospital visits to the University of Iowa Children's Hospital.

- Having grown up the son of a pediatrician, the easy answer is that I want to do pediatrics because that's all I know. I am really comfortable working with children and their parents. Where some of my classmates are naturals in the OR, I am at my best when I'm telling toddlers jokes so they are not scared of the doctor, or explaining nutrition to a new mother. Also, I feel that in pediatrics you can positively affect your patients for the rest of their lives. The most frustrating thing about my medicine rotation was that the chronic illnesses were mostly caused by the parents' own behavior. Emphysema, obesity, and diabetes all could be prevented by modifying their behavior. As a pediatrician I want to be a role model and instill lifelong habits into my patients, like exercising, eating right, and not smoking, so that they won't develop these problems in the future. Plus, they are the cutest population, and there is nothing that puts a smile on my face more than a twelve-month-old yelling "hello" as soon as I walk into a room.

- Medicine interests me because I have always been fascinated by and excelled in science. I feel that I can better utilize my knowledge and my experiences – as an intern for the Child Abuse Council and as a volunteer with victims of domestic violence – to help others than through any other career. I have been passionate about pursuing a medical career due to my interaction with physicians. As a child, I frequented doctor's offices due to my asthma and my blindness in one eye. I quickly noticed that the suggestions of these professionals led to great changes in my life and the betterment of my health. I knew that I, too, wanted to improve the health of others.

3. Why would you like to attend medical school here?

- I have always been able to adapt what I learned from past experiences to new challenges. SIU School of Medicine's focus on teamwork, problem-based learning, and serving the Illinois community perfectly complements what I wish to pursue in my life as a physician. I am especially interested in joining SIU's Psychiatry Interested Group and one of their many community outreach programs. I believe SIU's innovative learning methods, friendly learning atmosphere, and emphasis on community service would mold me into both a leading scientist and compassionate physician.

- As a PA student, one has roughly two to three years to become a highly knowledgeable, well-trained healthcare provider. So I want to be part of a program that I feel has the resources to prepare me to become the best PA possible in that short period of time. I truly feel Rush is that program. I like the fact that Rush offers an extra nine months of advanced practice rotations. I feel this will provide me with an incredible opportunity to solidify my clinical skills and prepare me to become an incredibly well-trained PA coming out of the program. I'm also fascinated with the practitioner-teacher model implemented here.

- This school is one of the top medical schools in the country with a challenging curriculum and renowned teachers. U of I's Center for Global Health allows me the ability to continue pursuing a career in global health and provides several opportunities to gain international experience, all of which I value in a medical school.

- Rush is a school that is known for its development of good clinical physicians. In my medical school research, I was looking for schools that would best prepare me for a career in primary care medicine. What really drew my attention to Rush was the Rush Community Service Initiatives Program. The variety of programs to participate in is impressive. On the website I saw many clinical and non-clinical programs, as well as the option for students to establish a new program or develop a project within the program. I like that these programs are designed to help in underserved communities. Working in the ER this year has shown me that understanding and treating patients from these communities can be challenging. Increased exposure to culturally diverse communities will make my provision of care better. This program also speaks well of the Rush medical community. Although community service is optional, more than 80 percent of students are participants in the program. I am looking to be part of a community that is enthusiastic and interactive. This program seems like a great way to get to know faculty members, students, and other members of the community while doing something that is good for the community.

- I have been privileged to have received Jesuit education for the past eight years at Loyola Academy and Georgetown and would love to attend a medical school with the Jesuit learning philosophy. Talking with my friends who have not had the same opportunity, I know there is something special that comes with the Jesuit philosophy of education. Receiving my training at Loyola will give me more than medical knowledge and procedural adequacy. The Jesuit values of commitment to justice and love will give me the foundation I need to not lose sight of the humanity of each patient. I am drawn to Loyola because of its emphasis on empathy for and connection to our fellow man. I hope to improve the medical experience for patients by imparting this philosophy into my practice.

As far as Loyola's campus features, I am intrigued and excited about the collaborative learning center. From what I understand, it has a six-bed virtual hospital that will be built like a clinical skills hospital and a simulated home care environment. I read that the building is supposed to be completed by the beginning of next year, and I would be thrilled to have an opportunity to do full hospital simulations before rotations. I like the idea of medical students, nursing students, and other healthcare professional students working together and sometimes independently in a controlled environment to simulate hospital situations. This building would be extremely helpful in developing and refining my clinical skills and learning how to collaboratively work with peers in the hospital.

- I really like Case Western's clinical affiliates – the University Hospitals' Level I Adult and Pediatric Trauma centers will provide a large and varied exposure during clinical rotations. Also, I'm quite interested in several of the combined degree programs offered at Case, including the PhD in health care management and the MBA. Plus, I've heard amazing things about the school, its professors, and its teaching style from an MIT alumna who's an M3 at your school. Finally, I'm quite excited about Case Western's curriculum. I consider myself a very self-directed learner, and the WR2 curriculum and case inquiries sound like an amazing way to learn.

- Rush would be my first choice for medical school because of the many advantages that it offers. They have both academic and community physicians. I have spoken to my brother and some of his friends and they have told me how approachable the teachers are and how participative the classes are at Rush. Everyone whom I have spoken with who attended Rush Medical School seemed to enjoy the relationships with their professors, as well as the varied clinical experiences that were offered. I'm very interested in the Rush Community Service Initiatives Program. Volunteer work is a big part of my life, and the ability to continue doing it through Rush will be a great privilege. Also, the advances in medicine people at Rush are working toward are fascinating. One of my brother's friends is currently doing research with the head of the Oncology Department. She injects strands of DNA with vaccines and exposes them to cancer cells to see the effects in the hope of finding vaccines to prevent cancer. I would love to get the opportunity to participate in research such as this. Although the professors and the other students are the most important things, I'm very impressed Rush scored so high in *US News* and *World Report*. I think it would be exciting to work at a new building at Rush.

- Rush: I want to go to Rush for a variety of reasons. First, I am so comfortable at Rush. Having gone to medical school there, I know the staff, the hospital, the residents, and the computer system. I know the strengths and I also know that I will get great training at Rush. One of the most important things about Rush is that the residents are working directly with the subspecialists managing a wide variety of patients. There are no fellows to act as go-betweens. Also there is a lot of interesting pathology that I have seen at Rush. There are also a lot of bread-and-butter peds, which is important because I plan on becoming a general pediatrician. Finally, Rush has a great outpatient clinic. The attendings there are wonderful. They are always accessible, patient, and willing to teach whenever they get the chance. It's also the most busy outpatient clinic of the city hospitals, so that will help hone my skills for the future.

- Lutheran: There are many things that drew me to Lutheran when I did my rotation there in the NICU. First off, the new facilities are incredible. Yacktman is pristine, and the patient rooms are amazing. Lutheran has a really busy census, and I am looking for a program that is busy. Having said that, the residents do not seem overworked, and they are all friendly and eager to teach. They helped me out in the NICU but also let me have independence with my own patients. They weren't constantly looking over my shoulder. In addition, the outpatient clinic is tremendously busy with wonderful attendings that are eager to teach and are great role models. This will be beneficial because I want to do outpatient general pediatrics.

- Loyola: There are many things that drew me to Loyola. First off, it has a community hospital feel to it. The classes are small and it seems that the residents and attendings are very close to one another. Another aspect that appealed to me was the curriculum. The wide variety of experiences that the residents get is broader than other programs. For example: During the first year, there are only four inpatient months and months on cardiology, adolescent medicine, and even surgery or anesthesia. Other programs have a higher emphasis on inpatient wards, so since I want to do outpatient medicine, this will benefit me greatly. I like all the simulations and crash courses that are offered so that we can practice our practical skills. I have not had the opportunity to do as many procedures as I have wanted during medical school, and this will be a great opportunity to do them.

- Rainbow Babies: There are many things that drew me to Rainbow. First off, it's on the forefront of technology and has amazing facilities to provide the best patient care. In addition, it is extremely busy. The outpatient clinic and the inpatient clinic are always teeming with patients, and this provides a great way to learn pediatrics. Also, it will help prepare me for life as a general pediatrician in a busy practice. One thing that particularly caught my eye was the emphasis of education on the part of the residents. I have always loved teaching. I was a TA in college, and as a fourth-year student have tried to teach the third-year students as much as I could when they were on my service. I hope one day to have medical students work in my office and teach them as much as I can.

- U of A: There are many things that drew me to U of A. First off, I really like the small class size. It gives each resident more autonomy when caring for the patient and makes them step into the physician role earlier than in larger programs. Also, I really like the diverse patient population at U of A. I minored in Spanish and really want to improve that aspect of my care. I can effectively communicate with patients now but want to be at a level where I don't need to call a translator on complicated cases. Another area that interests me is desert medicine. I really enjoy being outdoors, and wilderness and adventure medicine has always interested me. Finally, the Global Health Initiative is something I have always wanted to participate in.

- UCLA: One thing that immediately drew me to UCLA was the different training sites that residents work at. The different sites allow for the "total package" when learning ped's. At Mattel you do subspecialty work, at Cedars Sinai there is more traditional ped's, and at Santa Monica-UCLA there is a mix of the two. Working at each place with its unique patient population and different pathology allows for a well-rounded experience in all aspects of general ped's. The patient population that UCLA serves is very important to me. I really want to enhance my Spanish-speaking skills to better serve that population. The large class size is also an advantage because it allows the opportunity to work as a team and learn something from each resident. One thing I really liked was that even though it is a big class, all the residents know each other and you don't feel lost in the crowd.

- Stanford: One of my friends is a first-year resident there, and the thing she loves most about Stanford is that it has a small-program feel even though it's a relatively large program. There are multiple sites to work at, and each one has its positives. The community outreach is what drew me to Stanford the most, especially since I'm leaning toward specializing in primary care. There is such a good balance of subspecialty work with primary care that each resident gets the best training and is ready to excel in pediatrics upon graduating.

- Oregon: One of the things that drew me to Oregon was the size of their program. With only fifteen residents in a class, it seems like there is individualized attention between residents and attendings, which will help foster each resident in his or her career. Also, the hospital has a large census and thus provides a lot of independent work for each resident. One of the most important things for residents is to learn how to handle patients on their own because when they are done with their residency, they won't have attendings to fall back on. I pride myself on being able to handle patients by myself without the help of senior classmen, so I welcome the opportunity to work with a large and complicated patient load. Also, it seems like there is a large emphasis on resident well-being, and Oregon has both mountain and ocean, which provides a great outlet for things to do when not in the hospital.

- SLU: The first thing that drew me to SLU was the CARE program. During medical school, I volunteered at a free clinic called NLVS, which served mostly the underserved South Asian community. This was one of the clinics in which we were to work, and the most frustrating thing was that we only needed a $25,000 budget to operate for one full year, offering both free prescription medications and basic lab services, while other clinics were operating on multi-million dollar budgets. It was really an eye-opener to see how people couldn't even afford their diabetes medicine because it was more important for them to feed their families. I feel that the CARE program will help and is a great way to show future physicians how to handle barriers to healthcare. In the future I want to volunteer at free clinics to help provide care for less fortunate families. In addition, I really like the size of the program, which allows close interaction between attendings and residents. Coming from a smaller medical school, I think a small residency program fits my personality best.

- Children's: The thing that drew me to Children's was the opportunity to work in one of the most prestigious programs and hospitals in the country. Children from all over the world go to Children's for the quality of their care. This allows the residents to see the most unique pathology and routine pathology presenting in different ways. However, even though there are a lot of rare cases, there are a lot of bread-and-butter pediatrics that happen in the hospital, and it is this blend of common and rare that will benefit me most in my practice. Also, there is a strong emphasis on outpatient medicine, which I am leaning toward. Half the graduates end up working in general pediatrics, and with all the subspecialty training, I will feel more comfortable handling these cases myself rather than referring to a specialist.

TYPICAL QUESTIONS ASKED DURING INTERVIEWS

(Questions Provided by Prior Students)

- Tell me about yourself.
- Why do you want to be a physician?
- Why do you want to come to _____ for medical school?
- If asked to describe you, name three things your friends would say.
- What do you do to de-stress?
- Say you're on an airplane and the man next to you is starting to panic at the thought of flying – what would you do?
- Define empathy.
- What are some of the problems facing health care today?
- What is the most important issue in health care today?

- Tell me about a time you had to deal with your own preconceived notions or prejudices against someone.
- What are your greatest challenges? (Then followed up with questions specific to my response.)
- Describe one benefit technology brings to medicine and one negative impact technology may have on medicine.
- Tell me about your community service.
- Describe your research.
- What will you do if you aren't accepted to medical school?
- What books do you like/have you read recently?
- What are your hobbies? What do you do in your spare time?
- What are your accomplishments?
- Describe yourself and your work ethic.
- What do you think makes a good doctor? Why would you be a good doctor?
- What are your strengths?
- What are your weaknesses?
- What would you want to change/improve about yourself?
- If I asked someone who doesn't like you about you, what would they say?
- Describe your research in layman's terms. Would you consider doing this during your residency?
- Where have you enjoyed traveling?
- What will your obituary say?
- What do you like about this school?
- Tell me about your family.
- What do you think about HMO/PPOs?
- How do you feel about health care reform?
- What is your ideal day?
- What would you like to add to your application?
- How would a friend describe you?
- Describe a time when you failed.
- What was a difficult negative experience you have encountered?
- Why dentistry?
- What exposure do you have to dentistry?
- How have you reached out to the community and educated people about oral health?
- What is a challenge you have faced and how did you handle it?
- Describe a time you have worked in a group. How did you deal with the different personalities?

- Describe a time you were unable to fulfill a task.
  How did you handle the consequences?
- How do you prioritize your time if you have many things to do?
- Describe a time in which you took on a leadership role.
- Describe a time you went beyond expectations.
- What first made you interested in medicine?
- Have you considered any other healthcare professions,
  specifically nursing or physician assistant?
- How do you think you can apply your interests to being a better physician?
- Have you had any experience being in a group where there
  were differing races, cultures, or religions, and how were
  you able to navigate through those differences?
- What subspecialty do you see yourself pursuing? Why?
- What roles do you associate with a physician? (Educator, healer...)
- What was the main event/experience that convinced
  you that you wanted to be a physician?
- Where do you see yourself in 10 years? Please be specific,
  i.e., practicing in a private office, hospital...
- Discuss your strengths and how those pertain to practicing medicine.
- Based on your shadowing experiences, what would you mirror from
  the physicians you observed and what would you try to not mirror?
- How do you function within a group? As a leader or follower?
- Give an example of how you played a leadership role.
- What do you like to do in your spare time?
- What questions do you have about the program?
- Why do you think you score lower on tests than other individuals?
- What are your hobbies?
- Tell me about your family background and how that has shaped your life.
- How would you study for boards, since there are no tests/
  quizzes/study materials like there were in medical school?
- What do you do on the weekend before a big test?
- What would you do if you didn't get into dermatology?
- Why community health?
- At your college, did you ever feel like a number
  among forty thousand students?
- Tell me about your volunteering and the scholarship you won.
- What have you done to improve your GPA, because there is such
  a difference between beginning of college and end of college?
- Tell me about your MCAT score.

- Do you have a specialty in mind?
- Of all the applicants we get, why should we choose you?
- State a time where you had to make a really important decision quickly with little information.
- Do you feel that the government should fund more dental students than any other students, law, or engineers? State pros and cons.
- How can you overcome the conflicts that are associated with being a doctor?
- How do you overcome stress?
- What does it mean to be a leader for you?
- What has given you the reason to want to be part of the medical field?
- Who has been a major inspiration in your choice of medicine?
- Why is UMKC a major school on your list?
- How do you address failure?
- Do you believe medicine is a science or an art?
- What area in medicine do you want to major in and why?
- Who has motivated you to become involved with science?
- How can you keep up with a six-year BA/MD program?
- How can you make a difference in patient's lives?
- What are the key necessities a doctor must have?
- How has volunteering at the hospital been significant for you?
- Tell me about your current job.
- What do you think makes a good doctor?
- Go into more detail about the research paper you mention on your application.
- We have hundreds of applicants as qualified as you. What is it about you that should make us choose you over them?
- Did your parents ever try talking you out of pursuing medicine?
- What are some problems you see in medicine and health care?
- What can you bring to medicine?
- Why are you a good fit for Loyola?
- What will you do if you do not get into medical school this year?
- Talk about a challenge that you had to overcome.
- Talk about a time when you had difficulty adjusting to a situation. Why did you have difficulty?
- What are some problems in medicine today?
- Discuss a time when you were misjudged and how you overcame it.
- Talk about a challenge that you had to overcome.
- What do you do for fun?
- What are two strengths and weaknesses of yours?
- What is your greatest achievement?

- Define failure.
- Define success.
- When have you failed?
- I see you went to Adlai Stevenson High School, please tell me what you know about Adlai Stevenson.
- I see you went to John Kennedy High School, please tell me what you know about John Kennedy.
- I see you went to Dwight Eisenhower High School, please tell me what you know about Dwight Eisenhower.
- What makes having compassion or being compassionate important?
- Have you considered other medical fields?
- If you cannot be a doctor what will you do?
- Tell me more about your time in Japan.
- Is studying abroad something that is still important to you? Why?
- Tell me more about what you have been doing recently.
- Describe cultural diversity in your life and why it is important to you.
- Medical school is a marathon; how will you make it through?
- How will you/do you handle disappointment?
- How will you/do you handle stress?
- How important are your social support systems?
- Do you believe in mandated donated service for doctors?
- "Fun Question"...If I gave you a blank canvas, what would you paint?
- Tell me about your path to get here.
- Tell me more about your past work experiences.
- Where do you see yourself (medically/as a physician) in twenty years?
- Are you optimistic or pessimistic on health care reform?
- Is health care reform on a positive trajectory?
- How are technology and other changes in the world addressing the issues in regard to health care reform?
- What would your friends say about you?
- Please give three words/attributes that describe you.
- How would these attributes make you a good doctor?
- What are your best strength and your greatest weakness?
- What are your thoughts about other campuses at the U of I?
- What do you do when you get frustrated?
- What do you think is lacking in our health care system?
- What is the health care system like in Hong Kong?
- Why would we pick you?
- Tell me about your high school.

- What is your favorite activity?
- What do you think a typical Northwestern student is?
- If you could visit one place in the world, where would it be and why?
- If you could walk on water forever or fly three separate times, which would you choose and why?

THE INTERVIEW EXPERIENCE FROM A STUDENT'S PERSPECTIVE

I had my interview with Loyola Stritch School of Medicine and it went incredibly well. They were very friendly, and the interview style was very laid-back. When I arrived, the people at the admissions office handed me my itinerary for the day, which consisted of two interviews at 9:30 and 11:00 a.m., each one hour long. After that I took a tour with a first-year med student, had lunch, and then sat with some other students for a while in the Medical Center Commons area.

My first interview was with a doctor from the Pediatric Neonatology Unit. He brought me into his office, and we never really went through any formalities. We began talking, and the interview was more of a back-and-forth conversation than a question/answer session. I would say he spent just as much time talking as I did. He asked me about my dad, who graduated from Loyola, and we went from there. We covered everything on my application, and most of his questions pertained directly to what he read on my application. He asked about my trip with Global Medical Brigades, my research with Dr. M., and what kind of doctor I wanted to be. It was very informal, and I could tell he just wanted to get to know me. He did ask why I did not follow my dad's career path into dentistry, and thanks to you I had a great answer prepared. There were no questions that were out of the blue. His question style was along the lines of, "So, tell me about your experience with *blank* organization."

My second interview was with a resident in the Pediatric Unit. She graduated from U of I, as did my first interviewer. We had a lot in common, and our interview, again, was conversational. She brought me into a room with a small round table in the back of the Admissions Office, and she began with a question straight off of my application. We talked about similar things that I talked about in my first interview, but we also talked about life outside of school, and she told me how she balances her career with a personal life. She asked about my hobbies and what I like to do outside of the classroom. Again, she took all of her questions straight off of my application, and nothing caught me off-guard.

Neither interviewer, at any point, asked me something like, "Tell me about a leadership experience," or, "What makes you special for our school?" I was very nervous leading up to the interview, but I was not nervous at all once the whole process started.

At one point, the head of admissions came and talked with the group of interviewees. He gave us a short run-down of what Loyola is all about and what student life is like. Then he said that Loyola wants students who want to be there, and he asked us each why we chose to apply to Loyola. I had a feeling that he did this with all students who interview, so I would recommend to anyone else applying to Loyola to come up with a good answer to that question. I referred to their mission statement in my answer. I said that Loyola's mission statement says that the school's priorities lie in service, compassion, and respect for human life. I said that when I think of practicing medicine, those are the things that immediately come to mind.

Feedback from another student:
In the interviews, I was asked the thee questions you told me, as well as various random questions, such as what epitaph I would want my tombstone, what I do for fun, and what will be the biggest challenge I will face in medical school.

CHALLENGING INTERVIEW QUESTIONS

Increasingly, students are being asked what they think about health care reform. Despite the Supreme Court's decision, this is an area in which I don't want to provide advice because if a student states an opinion on the issue, and the interviewer doesn't agree, the student is in trouble.

Nonetheless – and again, despite the Supreme Court having ruled – here's a question every medical school candidate had better be prepared to answer (and some suggested answers):

- What do you think about Obamacare?

I would recommend considering the following questions and suggested answers:

1. **What is Obamacare? (Please note, only opponents of PPACA refer to the health care reform act this way.)**

   Answer: It is sweeping health care reform legislation that is complicated and may have unintended consequences. Only time will tell. Key provisions are intended to extend coverage to millions of uninsured Americans; to implement measures that will lower healthcare costs while at the same time increasing quality and efficiency; and to eliminate insurance industry practices such as rescission and denial of coverage due to pre-existing conditions.

2. What do Republicans say?

Answer: "Obamacare" is unconstitutional due to the individual mandate provision, which requires all Americans to purchase health insurance. It places an undue burden on small business and will cost Americans more healthcare dollars, not less. Congress is overreaching into the private affairs/decisions of American citizens. Recently, when "Obamacare" was challenged in the Supreme Court, the legislation was upheld.

3. What do Democrats say?

Answer: Health care is a fundamental right for all Americans. Since persons who are uninsured are basically cared for on the backs of insured Americans, it is only fair that all persons be required to carry insurance, but it must be made accessible and affordable for Americans on all ends of the economic spectrum. PPACA will save lives, as ample research demonstrates that the uninsured die from every cause at a much higher rate, and health care reform will begin to control healthcare costs.

4. What is a neutral statement?

Answer: I support certain aspects of the act, but have reservations about others. For example, I think it is good that more people will have access to insurance, but I worry about the costs. Also, I think that while it is important to make health care more efficient and to have high quality outcomes, I hope it doesn't interfere with the relationship between doctors and patients. I think all of us will have to work cooperatively over a long period of time to ensure that America's health care remains the best in the world.

If you find yourself in a situation where you must answer, I would recommend a neutral statement.

A corollary question is whether access to quality medical care is a right or a privilege. Again, this is based on the perspective of the interviewer, and I don't see how you can provide a response without the risk of getting into trouble. The most neutral response I can suggest in regard to whether health care is a right or a privilege is to try and land somewhere in the middle. For example, you could say, "I believe that everyone should be able to receive the medical treatment they need, but I understand there are unlimited legitimate needs and limited resources."

ANOTHER GOOD ANSWER TO YET ANOTHER GOOD QUESTION

- Why didn't you go to medical school directly after graduation?

I have talked with my father often about his medical school experiences, and from what he tells me, when clinical rotations began in his class, there was a noticeable difference between students who had previous clinical experience and those who did not. He said that he could always tell who had clinical experience because those students were more comfortable and confident in their patient interactions. Although I had experience as an EMT, I wanted more practical experience with doctors. I found a great opportunity to do this with my job as an emergency room scribe. As a scribe I get to see a variety of interesting medical cases and observe how doctors handle different types of patients. One of the more acute cases I saw was of a mentally retarded infant who came into the ER in critical condition. Due to the infant's age and condition, a group of doctors dropped what they were doing to evaluate the infant and figure how to best handle the delicate situation. The doctor I was scribing for managed to intubate the infant and lower his breathing rate from over sixty breaths per minute to a normal rate. Situations like these show me how I should handle myself when I eventually start clinical rotations.

ETHICAL QUESTIONS

When I first started this process nine years ago, it seemed like many schools asked the same ethical question over and over again: what would you do if you saw a student cheating? If it were me, I would say I would mind my own business, but that's not the politically correct answer. The politically correct answer is, "I would confront the person and tell him that if he didn't admit he was cheating, then I would have to report him."

Another example of an ethical question one of my students was asked went something like this: Your future husband's parents have never liked you and don't want their son to marry you. You have a difficult time with them, and two weeks before your wedding ceremony, they send you an extremely expensive mahogany bedroom set, dining room set, and living room set. What do you say to your in-laws? My response would have been, "Thank you very much." Then the medical school interviewer says, "Well I'm going to tell you that mahogany is a banned substance, and it's against the law to utilize it. Now what would you tell your in-laws?" My response would be, "Well if I refuse it, it's not going to grow back in the rainforest, so I would simply make a donation within my means to the organization that saves mahogany or the rain forest." Would this have satisfied the interviewer? I don't know. Below are other examples of ethical questions to consider.

1. You are working as a resident, and a doctor tells you to order tests for a patient. You realize two hours later, after other tests come back, that you left out one of the tests that the doctor told you to order. You have had a lot of experience with these types of patients and know what the course of action to treat the patient will be. What do you do?

2. A patient goes to the doctor for a regular checkup, and the patient tells him about some problem he has been having (chest pain). Due to the patient's family history and complaint, the doctor tells the patient, who is a heavy smoker, that he has to quit smoking. The patient is uncooperative and does not stop. Smoking helps him relieve the stress he has from working two jobs to support his wife and eight kids. Sometime later the patient files a malpractice lawsuit against the doctor because a blood clot was discovered in his leg. The patient blames the doctor for not making him quit smoking. How would you have acted as a physician to make sure the patient quit smoking?

3. One of your patients is in a coma and is on life support. You have had several different specialists come in to evaluate the patient and they all report that the patient's condition is not going to improve. The specialists believe that the patient should be taken off life support but the family does not want to do that. What do you do in this situation?

4. Discuss a time when you have had an ethical dilemma.

5. You're late to surgery clinic due to bad weather, and the attending has already excised a site. She tells you to close on your own and leaves the room. After you finish suturing, you realize that the site is the wrong one. What do you do?

6. Under what circumstances would you consider stealing a loaf of bread? What are the cons? What can a person steal in modern times that would be comparable to bread?

7. How can you overcome the ethics of medicine within the coming years?

8. How do you address a financial situation with a poor patient and a rich patient?

9. Do you judge a patient?

10. Do you believe in giving a placebo to a patient?

CHAPTER 9

RESIDENCY

Similar to applying to medical school, it's helpful to know what you want to do for a specialty early in your medical school experience. In this way, you can do your optional electives in the field, hopefully at schools that you prefer.

It's clear that, just like anyone else, residency programs like to hire people they know. It makes all the sense in the world, and the people they know are the people who do their elective rotations there. Therefore, the people who decide what they want to do after they complete their elected rotations are put at a disadvantage.

The questions and process for residency, other than having done research and rotations in the area that you want to be a resident in, are basically the same three questions you prepared for applying to medical school:

1. Tell me about yourself.
2. Why do you want to be a *blank*?
3. Why do you want to do your residency here at *blank*?

It wouldn't hurt if you performed some research or co-authored an article in the specialty you are interested in.

For those factors mentioned above, it's important to have a high class rank and to have done well on the National Boards.

Many medical school students ask me for advice regarding which residency they should pursue, both in terms of lifestyle and remuneration. I advise them that they are making a decision today that might not take effect for many years, and in the interim, the market can change.

In the early '90s, the government and many of the healthcare pundits were predicting the growth in power and remuneration for primary care physicians at the expense of subspecialists. I remember in 1994 and 1995, I received numerous calls from gastroenterologists, cardiologists, radiologists, and anesthesiologists who were willing to perform primary care in a clinic because they could not find a position in their chosen specialty. Later in the late '90s, and continuing through today, all of these specialties – gastroenterology, cardiology, radiology, pathology – have been in high demand and have very high rates of remuneration.

I have seen several medical students who could have selected any specialty they wanted and would most likely have been approved, but who wanted to be pediatricians. This was their passion, this is what they felt would be rewarding in their lives, and they didn't care about lifestyle or financial remuneration. For those looking for more of a financial reward, it's hard to go wrong, at least for the foreseeable future, and based on past history, being an "Ologist": e.g., radiologist, pathologist, anesthesiologist, dermatologist, otolaryngologist, ophthalmologist, hematologist, oncologist, or cardiologist.

Emergency Department medicine, both for adult and pediatrics, is currently very popular because the individual does not have to wear a beeper; does not have to worry about being a businessperson, unless directing the group; and can have a flexible schedule.

I have said several different times in this book that you should never mention that you want to attend a medical school or do a residency because of its location, as I believe this would be like a girl telling a boy, "I really don't like you but I like your car," or a girl telling the last boy at the dance, "You're ugly and stupid but there's no one left."

I therefore feel that you should never mention it. However, truth be told, when I attended a specific class on selecting your residency (many hospital administration programs do have a residency), the professor directing the class was discussing in depth the merits of different types of residencies, such as working with a health plan, an insurance company, long-term care, a consulting firm, Certificate of Need Board, or a hospital. I remember saying, "I don't care where I go as long as it's Chicago." The professor was outraged and said, "If Dr. J., PhD, the director of the program, heard what you said, you would be terminated from the graduate program." I walked myself into Dr. J.'s office and said, "In our class for selecting a residency, I indicated to Dr. L. that I didn't care where I went or what I did as long as it was Chicago." I said, "Furthermore, Dr. L. said you would kick me out of the program if you knew I said this." Fortunately for me, Dr. J. was a kind, gentle, helpful soul and said, "I think I have a friend at Lutheran General Hospital in Park Ridge.

Is that near Chicago? Let me see if I can get you in there." He did, and I performed my administrative residency at Lutheran General Hospital.

Thank you, Dr. J.

Even though I am a hypocrite, please do what I say and not what I did, and don't say you want to go somewhere because of its location, weather, or baseball team.

AN EXAMPLE OF A GREAT PERSONAL STATEMENT FOR A RESIDENCY

One of the experiences that led me to pursue a career as an obstetrician/gynecologist occurred while working on the medical mobile van parked at 16th and Cicero. There was a woman who was recovering from a heroin addiction and was a victim of physical and sexual abuse. Cervical and breast cancer screening were far from her mind, as she was there for her Suboxone prescription and evaluation of a facial laceration. It is moments such as these that remind us of the unique problems that women face, and it is the importance of the bond between a female patient and her physician that propelled me into the field of OB/GYN.

OB/GYN is an ideal profession for me because it is a challenging field involving technical procedures, yet it also focuses on education, prevention, and a strong, long-lasting patient/physician relationship. This is one of the few specialties in which you can surgically treat a patient with cancer but also be on the forefront of cancer prevention in your outpatient clinic. This combination appeals to me, as I would be able to utilize all of my strengths. In addition, many medical specialties focus on pathological disease, whereas OB/GYN allows physicians to take part in an amazing physiologic process, pregnancy and childbirth. I am excited to be a part of such an important moment in my patients' lives, but I am also prepared to support my patients when the outcome is unexpected.

I have been drawn to women's health by the meaningful connections made during each patient encounter in clinics, in shelters, and throughout my third-year clerkships. While volunteering in the community during my pre-clinical years, I was disappointed to discover so many women who did not understand the importance of screening, had health misconceptions, or were afraid to seek care. I soon learned that by taking the time to educate patients in a clear and relevant manner, awareness of the importance of pap smears, mammography, prenatal care, and proper use of contraception could be greatly enhanced. Education and prevention became the focus of my community outreach, and it was at this time that I founded Original Change Project, an organization with the aim to provide health education and referrals to free health and social services within the community.

I also found my niche in preventive medicine through my instruction in an adolescent sexual health course, my research with the Chicago Breast Cancer Task Force, and my work on the medical mobile van. When I began my third-year clerkships, I discovered that misconceptions and a lack of information exist not only in the shelters and at health fairs at local food depositories, but are widespread, afflicting people of all ages, ethnicities, education, and socioeconomic levels. As a result of this, I have made it my goal to ensure that all my patients receive the proper education, support, screening, and health services needed to increase awareness of disease and enhance health and well-being within our community.

Throughout medical school I have displayed professionalism, dedication to academic achievement, and strength as a leader. More importantly, I have demonstrated a compassion and humanistic nature, which are valued qualities for an obstetrician/gynecologist to possess when dealing with such private medical concerns of patients. I am open-minded, compassionate, and dedicated to providing my patients with the best care possible. I have been honored by my classmates with induction into the Gold Humanism Honor Society for my dedication to service. While I deeply appreciate their recognition, the greatest honor is spending time to educate and support my patients. The phrase "patient advocate" has appeared several times on my evaluation. I take great pride in this, as I always do whatever is in my power to ensure that my patients are receiving the care that they deserve. I believe that the combination of compassion and determination for great patient care will serve me well as an obstetrician/gynecologist.

Looking back at that night on the mobile van, if I were her physician, I would be able to provide her with pre-natal care, deliver her children, provide appropriate screening, and intervene surgically if necessary. Most importantly, I would be able to support her through her drug rehabilitation and provide her with every resource possible to better her personal and social situation. It is the diversity of this specialty and the unique nature of the patient population and medical concerns that have influenced me to enter the field of OB/GYN. When evaluating my goals as a physician along with my experiences, strengths, and attributes, I believe that I could make a valuable contribution to the residency program and the medical field, merging all of my strengths in order to provide the best care possible to my patients.

Comment: *I had a few grammatical changes only.*

ONE STUDENT'S PREPARATION FOR RESIDENCY

Tell me about yourself.

I was born in Scotland. My dad's training had us move around a lot, and I spent time in the United Kingdom, Saudi Arabia and Canada before moving to the United States. I have been living around Chicago for some time now, excluding the four years I spent in college, when I went to the University of Illinois at Urbana-Champaign and studied finance. I have an older sister who's a marketing professional and a younger brother in high school. When I'm not at school, I am pretty religious about going to the gym, and I enjoy golfing. My biggest passion outside of medicine is food. I love exploring new cuisines in Chicago, and the food scene is usually the first place I check out in a new city.

Why do you want to be a radiologist?

My interest for radiology developed during anatomy class my first year. At the time I really enjoyed learning anatomy and correlating it with plain films and CTs. After that I spent some time with radiologists at Loyola and grew fascinated with their utilization of technology, and their fluency in the diagnosis and treatment of pathology from head to toe. I liked that when radiologists go over a study, they more or less start out with a blank slate. Although they may have some history, once they open up a study they can find just about anything, and they have to go back and put together a diagnosis, or multiple problems, almost like a puzzle. But what makes radiology truly meaningful to me is what I saw during my third year when I rotated through all my clerkships, and I saw how all of these clinicians, in vastly different fields, based their care on the interpretations and recommendations given by radiologists. Being able to utilize such a large amount of knowledge to partake in the care of such a wide variety of patients is what brings me to the field.

Why do you want to go to _____ (fill in the name of the school that you are applying for).

For academic programs:

Part of the reason I like radiology is because of how innovative the field is. There is continuous research and advancements being made at the physics level, in designing new equipment, and developing new indications and studies with the available technology. With so much innovation going on, I want to join an academic program so that I can find my own area of interest, and work alongside distinguished mentors to make my own contributions to the field while in residency. A few particular things I like about this program are…(*will fill in once I know where I will be interviewing*).

For community programs:

Part of the reason I like radiology is how fluent radiologists are in illnesses from head to toe. In the future I want to be a radiologist who can interpret any study, perform a wide array of radiologic procedures, and partake in the care of patients across all services in the hospital and outpatient clinics. With this goal in mind, I want to come to a community program where I will be able to get ample hands-on experience alongside great teachers so that I can leave residency with the knowledge and confidence to be an all-encompassing asset at my future hospital. When I was selecting programs to apply to, I wasn't looking for flashy names or fancy cities but rather programs that will provide me with the ample training needed to be a competent radiologist. A few specific things I like about this program are...(*will fill in once I know where I will be interviewing*).

Comment: *Very good. This person knew he wanted to be a radiologist before medical school, so he took radiology electives and participated in radiology research.*

CHAPTER 10

COULD THE PRINCIPLES IN THIS BOOK APPLY TO PREPARING FOR INTERVIEWS FOR OTHER POSITIONS?

Yes, particularly the questions "Tell me about yourself" and "Why would you like to work at this organization?" This would involve the same type of dedication to learning about your potential employer, but should also include what you can do for the employer.

Good preparation equals good luck.

SO, YOU
WANT TO BE
A PHYSICIAN?

CHAPTER 11

WHAT IF YOU DON'T GET IN?

There are several master's programs available, such as a Master of Science in biology/chemistry at Loyola or at Bennington College in Vermont, that offer a post-bachelor, pre-medical education degree. The Bennington College program offers two courses over twelve months, ten months of them being academic courses in biology and chemistry, and then two months preparing for the MCATs. They allegedly have a high medical school acceptance rate. Their phone number is 802-440-4885, and the website for their program is: http://www.bennington.edu/Academics/GraduateCertificatePrograms/Postbac/Postbac.aspx

John Hopkins University also has a post-baccalaureate premedical program. Their telephone number is 410-516-7748. Their website is www.jhu.edu/postbac.

Other options include getting new experiences, e.g., being a scribe in an Emergency Department or performing research. Or, if it was the MCATs that hurt you, receive tutoring or retake the Kaplan course.

Or if you didn't take them before, take them now.

CHAPTER 12

OTHER ALTERNATIVES

When students ask me about being a doctor of osteopath, or going to a foreign medical school, I respond with the following questions: "Do you know what they call an individual who finishes Harvard Medical School first in his or her class?" Response: "Doctor." "Do you know what they call the individual who finished last in his or her medical school class at Guadalajara?" Response: "Doctor." "Do you know what Medicare pays a primary care physician from Harvard who finished first in his or her class for a routine visit?" Response: "The same that they pay a primary care physician who finished last in his or her class at Guadalajara."

I don't personally find any difference between MDs and DOs, although some people might. Quite frankly, from my experience, it's just about as difficult to get into a DO school as an MD school.

What I have learned from students that applied to a DO school, and from an osteopathic physician on my medical staff who serves as an interviewer for one of the DO medical schools, is that DO schools look very favorably on those applicants who have only applied to DO schools. In other words, if you are applying to DO schools as a backup, they would take this as a negative. On the other hand, if you applied to all DO schools in different states, they would see that as a positive. Additionally, the two students that I coached who were accepted to DO schools both were thoroughly familiar with the history and philosophy of osteopathic medicine and were both passionate about it, and I am confident this was a very significant advantage to them in their acceptance.

Ultimately, class rank and medical school can have an impact on which residencies you can be accepted into.

Obviously, the foreign medical schools in my day were in Mexico, typically Guadalajara, but now there is a plethora of medical schools in the Caribbean, India, and Europe, which have easier criteria than American schools. An online search can quickly help find the right fit, but I have listed a few links below that might prove useful.

Mexico: http://www.iime.org/database/northam/mexico.htm
Caribbean: http://en.wikipedia.org/wiki/List_of_medical_schools_in_the_Caribbean
India: http://en.wikipedia.org/wiki/Medical_Schools_in_India
Europe: http://en.wikipedia.org/wiki/List_of_medical_schools_in_Europe

CHAPTER 13

OTHER HEALTH CARE–RELATED FIELDS

Much to my surprise, one of the physicians' sons called me and asked if he could go through the interview coaching process to become a physician assistant. The individual had a very decent grade point average (a 3.6 at Duke) and had an acceptable, but not great score on the MCATs (a 28). He interviewed very well. I asked him why he didn't want to go to medical school, and he indicated that he had given a great deal of thought to this and that if he did become a physician, he would most likely be a pediatrician. For approximately one-quarter the time in school, he would make almost as much being a physician assistant as a pediatrician, and he wouldn't have to carry a beeper or be a businessman. Additionally, because he already had an undergraduate degree, he could complete the program in two years. There are alternatives to being a physician, such as nurse practitioner, physician assistant, certified nurse midwife, and certified nurse anesthetist.

I would just highly recommend you don't become a hospital administrator, unless you're into sadomasochism.

CHAPTER 14

TESTIMONIALS

In all the years I have been advising medical school applicants, I have asked only one thing in return: that they write back to me and tell me about their trials, tribulations, and experiences in the application and – hopefully – acceptance process.

This chapter is a compilation of testimonials I have received over nine years of "coaching."

As a BA/MD applicant, I had little experience with interviews and thus was very nervous about my prospects. However, after working with Mr. Goldberg through a series of mock interviews and running my essays by him, I was given the confidence I needed to approach the application process with eagerness as opposed to a more reticent disposition. My gratitude toward Mr. Goldberg and his help is endless. In fact, I truly believe that had it not been for Mr. Goldberg's help, I would not have received as many BA/MD program acceptances as I did. I'm definitely hoping to work with him again when it comes time to apply for residency, and recommend his services to anyone considering a career in healthcare.

– Shani Chibber

———

I wanted to let you know that I matched at UIC for radiology. I was really excited to find this out a couple weeks ago. I meant to tell you earlier, but believe it or not, school has gotten much busier after Match Day rather than the smooth sailing till graduation I was hoping for. Thank you once again for all your interview and personal statement help. I felt pretty confident that I nailed my interviews. I look forward to future interactions and conversations with you.

– Senthil Gunasekaran

———

My conversations with Mr. Goldberg completely changed my outlook on interviewing. Previous to our first meeting, I assumed my natural conversational abilities would carry me through a dental school interview. When I sat down with Mr. Goldberg, he made me realize I was stumbling through my words while talking about my own life experiences. In just a few days, I was completely prepared to discuss the important parts of my pre-dental life. Additionally, Mr. Goldberg helped me improve my speaking skills and made sure I would be dressed to impress. I felt very confident and prepared for my interview. I am so thankful for the opportunity to be mentored by Mr. Goldberg. He has incredible insight into what it takes to ace an interview. Thank you again Mr. Goldberg!

— Colleen McShane

———

Meeting with Mr. Goldberg helped me tremendously in the interview process. After meeting with him, I felt that I had sharpened my ability to speak clearly and professionally while still conveying my personality and values. Although I was not sure what questions would be asked on interview day, I was more prepared to answer unexpected questions. I very much appreciate his help and would recommend interview training/practice to anyone working toward a career in medicine.

— Chelsey McShane

———

Hi! I just wanted to let you know that I was accepted to UIC. I just found out this weekend. I am very excited about it. I had an interview at Washington University in St. Louis two weeks ago, which went well. Thank you so much!

— Jori Sheade

———

I hope you are doing well! Senior year is coming to an end for me, and I am pleased to tell you that I will be attending UIC's GPPA Medical Program. I would like to thank you again for helping me during this application process. Your interview method and book were all extremely helpful!

— Carolyn Cao

———

I wanted to thank you again for helping me during the interviewing process. By practicing interview questions and skills with you, I felt more confident and comfortable during my own interviews, especially when challenging questions arose. I also learned appropriate etiquette and manners to use during the interview. Multiple interviewers commended me on my interview skills, and I have you to thank for that.

– Elie Schwartz

———

My name is James B. McShane, and I am a dentist on staff at Alexian Brothers Hospital. I have known Mr. Edward Goldberg since my four children were small. They are now in their late teens and early twenties and have begun to benefit from a rare and valuable talent Mr. Goldberg possesses, the ability to teach others how to conduct themselves during interviews for admission to professional schools.

Mr. Goldberg, president and CEO of St. Alexius Medical Center, once told me that he put a high value on young people and took great pride in helping deserving students achieve their dreams. He mentioned that so as not to be overwhelmed, he limited this coaching service to the children of the medical staff at St. Alexius and employees. This did not surprise me as Mr. Goldberg has a longstanding reputation for being physician- and employee-friendly. In 2010 my oldest child was granted several interviews for admission to dental schools. She had nice credentials but was uncertain about her interview skills. I met personally with Mr. Goldberg and asked him if he would help her. He not only agreed but invited me to sit out of sight and within earshot so I could get a feel for his technique and appreciate my daughter's improvement. The results were amazing. After a few rather intense sessions, she not only knew what was important to say but realized the significance of posture, eye contact, attire, and much more. About a month later, my second daughter was granted an interview for medical school. Mr. Goldberg generously afforded her the same attention. As you might guess, this story has a happy ending, as both my girls are currently concluding their first years of dental and medical school respectively.

Since then I have referred three more hopefuls to Mr. Goldberg. Interestingly, one had fine credentials but did not survive the interview phase of her application process to medical school two years earlier. Another was applying to a physician assistant program, and the most recent was attempting to gain admission to veterinary school. All three have been admitted, and it is my belief that their improved interview skills were a significant factor in their success. I also have two sons, both of which are interested in dentistry, and if they are fortunate enough to be granted interviews, you can be sure I will ask Mr. Goldberg to help them. I know he will help with any residency interviews as well.

The competition for seats in professional schools today is as fierce as it ever has been. Obviously, all these applicants had outstanding credentials to be granted interviews, but the odds are still tough at that point. Edward Goldberg's advice and encouragement have proven invaluable time after time, and I would like to personally thank him for his time and mostly for his concern for the future of medicine in our country.

– James B. McShane, DDS

———

Before I met Mr. Goldberg, I considered myself a naturally strong interviewer and public speaker. When I was rejected from my first medical school interview on my second attempt to pursue medicine, all of my confidence in interviewing was brought into question. It was a defeating feeling to realize my prior interviewing strategy was not effective; I knew I needed help. Mr. Goldberg helped me revise my strategy, keep some of my strengths, and work on new strengths.

When we first met in January 2011, he introduced new interviewing techniques that I had never considered before. At first, I was reluctant to introduce changes. Learning to prepare scripts for interview questions felt unnatural to me. When I overcame my stubbornness and used his method, they were effective and granted me two school acceptances. I do not intend to revert to my old habits ever again; I learned my lesson.

Mr. Goldberg helped me realize that I was coming across as an arrogant applicant with an attitude in my medical school interviews, which was not a true representation of my character. It certainly was not how I wanted to be remembered by interviewers. Mr. Goldberg set me straight in my mentality and taught me a valuable lesson about humility. I then accepted that I did not know it all and I was certainly not an expert. I was still a student when it came to interviewing, which was the first lesson I needed to learn. His teachings were the reality check I needed to pinpoint exactly why I wanted to pursue medicine, how to approach an interview, and how I wanted to present myself.

When interviewing with Mr. Goldberg, I was challenged to maintain a balance of confidence and humility. Even under pressure, I learned how to speak articulately and concisely. I knew I was a difficult student, set in my ways, and Mr. Goldberg continued to meet with me time after time. I could tell he was truly dedicated to help me the best that he could.

I was able to apply my new "Goldberg" interviewing skills in three medical school interviews. I was waitlisted at one school and accepted into the other two schools. I believe those acceptances were due to his contributions in molding me into a stronger interviewer. I was able to offer my best self in the interviews through my words, body language, and general presentation.

I intend to carry his teachings with me in future interviews for residency and beyond. This experience was a career-changing lesson, and I am eternally grateful.

– Joyce Jhang

———

I entered medical school immediately following my undergraduate education. As a result, I'd never had an interview for anything more than a part-time job. Although I had good grades, extracurricular activities, and research, I was inexperienced at interviewing. Given the importance of the interview in medical school admissions, I turned to Mr. Goldberg for help. With his help, I learned to smoothly integrate my strengths, such as my research experience, when responding to questions. In addition, he taught me important skills that can apply to all interviews and will undoubtedly help me in the future. Because of the help of Mr. Goldberg, I was calm and confident during my medical school interviews, and was successful in receiving an acceptance.

– Josh Newman

———

I believe that my acceptance into medical school was due, in large part, to the mentoring I received from Mr. Goldberg. Having the academic credentials to qualify for med school is just the starting point of a long, arduous process. Having no physicians in the family, I had no idea what to expect from the application process, which resulted in a number of esteem-crushing rejections. A family friend introduced me to Mr. Goldberg, who understood what I was going through, and although we had never met before, he agreed to help me achieve my dream.

As the president/CEO of a hospital, his candid advice and familiarity with the expectations of medical school admission was invaluable. His interviewing technique advice helped me ace my third and last interview with the University of Miami-Miller School of Medicine, where I was eventually accepted. This is why I believe strongly in Mr. Goldberg's mentorship. I went on the have a wonderful four-year experience at UM and matched at my first choice of residency programs, Northwestern Memorial Hospital in Chicago, where I will start in June 2012. Thank you to Mr. Goldberg for helping me achieve my goal.

– Veronica Penyak

———

I was aspiring to gain admission to a competitive direct admission medical program from high school. With the help of Mr. Goldberg, I was able to achieve my goal. He gives individual training for interviews, and brought out the best in me. He taught me how to highlight my abilities, spirit, and commitment to medicine at a conversational, yet professional, level.

– Toral Vaidya

———

During my studies at the Medical College at Rush University, I had heard from others about Mr. Goldberg's superior coaching skills. So when the time came for me to apply for a residency in obstetrics, I felt confident that he was the right person to approach to help strengthen my application in the competitive rush for securing a residency. My instincts were spot on, and his excellent insight into the medical field and honest advice allowed me to hone in on the most important details to emphasize in my residency application personal statement.

After making the changes to the personal statement that Mr. Goldberg and I originally discussed, I continued to be impressed by his interest and commitment in assisting me with further refinement to my writing in subsequent drafts. While working with Mr. Goldberg, I found him to be kind, professional, and very effective. I feel his coaching played a big part in my success in gaining the residency I'd always hoped for, and I am grateful for his guidance. I would absolutely recommend Mr. Goldberg's tutoring to all medical school applicants, and those who are seeking their ideal residency match.

– Tara Usakoski

———

I met Mr. Goldberg at St. Alexius Hospital when I was there to implement the scribe program. He was very welcoming and enthusiastic about my ambition of becoming a physician. Aside from talking about medicine, which he is vastly passionate about, he is definitely someone who can hold a conversation with you about anything, including the color blue! His optimistic attitude and motivation to succeed influenced me to reach for the stars. Once I told him about applying to medical school I saw his desire to help me achieve the best and he offered to assist me with my essay writing. His advice on polishing my essay was immensely helpful. Furthermore, he gave me a different perspective on how to write my essays, and how to highlight my accomplishments without having to sound conceited. He has been a great influence on my acceptance into medical school, and I have been honored to have had the privilege of knowing him. He is definitely a great resource and played a strong force in my journey of becoming a physician.

–Afsha Rais

———

I was a special case, and probably a challenge, for Mr. Goldberg. I was offered his services late in the game. I had already taken the MCAT, written the personal statement and entrance essays, received letters of recommendation, and sent out applications to medical schools. In fact, by the time I started to converse with him, I had already scheduled two of my interviews. We had to act fast to perfect my presentation and my dialogue, involving writing out the answers to the three most frequently asked questions. In a matter of one afternoon, we went from the initial flawed version to a product that I liked and that Mr. Goldberg agreed was good. Although only one of the questions came up, I was prepared to answer the question, although it was asked in such a way that I could not use the script, it still allowed me to make sure to mention all of the key points.

I attended undergraduate school far away and I could not easily come home, so I was forced to meet him the morning of the day I was going to travel to Arizona for my interview. Although not the most convenient circumstances, I am glad that I was able to meet him in person. It was ironic that all of the areas I felt I was weaker in (eye contact, fluid speaking in interviews, etc.), Mr. Goldberg said I did nearly perfectly and the areas that I didn't think I needed to work on were the ones he said I needed to fix. He told me that my presence was among the best of all whom he had helped, which made me feel significantly more confident. That is the most important thing that I have taken from all of his assistance; the boost in confidence and the advice to change what was weak.

Although I did not get accepted to the school that he helped me with, I did get accepted into the school with the later interview date. I took what Mr. Goldberg told me as well as my experience with the first school and was able to apply it for the second one. I have since referred a couple people to his book, including a fellow student and my pre-medical adviser, who said she would research it and possibly use it for future students. I honestly wish I could have obtained his assistance a year or two earlier to benefit from all of the other information on MCAT preparation, mission statement critiques, and undergraduate advice, but in the end, I got into my dream medical school, so I am thankful for the assistance I received.

— Ashton Brunn

———

I wanted to let you know that I was accepted into the GPPA Program, and I would like to thank you for your help and time commitment as I was preparing for the interview. I was also accepted into the six-year BA/MD program at the University of Missouri – Kansas City, and I was able to translate some of the skills from our practice sessions to the interviews for that medical school as well. Again, thank you for all of your help; I really appreciate it!

— Eddy Nabrinsky

———

I cannot thank Mr. Goldberg enough for his help and knowledge in the application process to dental school. His professionalism demonstrates a genuine care and respect for anyone who walks through his door. While working with Mr. Goldberg, we focused on the interview process. He taught me professional and interview etiquette, and how to present myself in the best light. We collectively discussed my experience and volunteer work, and how to effectively communicate my passion for dentistry. He taught me what to emphasize during the interview and how to express it. Working with Mr. Goldberg was very beneficial in my preparation for interviews; I felt very prepared on the interview day. His advice and generosity met and exceeded my expectations. I highly recommend him to anyone who is looking to enter professional school.

– Elyse Zarek

———

When I first corresponded with Mr. Goldberg about interview tutoring, he asked me the question I had been dreading to answer: Why do you want to be a doctor? Don't get me wrong – being a physician will be a wonderful and fulfilling profession for me. However, the "why" had been very difficult for me to put into words. Not until I met with Mr. Goldberg was I able to verbalize my feelings toward the medical profession. Through collaborative discussion, a *lot* of drafts, and even more editing, I was able to really pinpoint what it was about being a doctor that made it the profession I needed to follow. Because of Mr. Goldberg's mentoring, I was successful during this application cycle, receiving invitations to four of the five medical schools with whom I interviewed.

– Tovah Schwartz

———

My interactions with Mr. Goldberg in preparation for on-campus interviews when seeking admission into medical school proved to be invaluable. With our first meeting, which began with him casually taking the time to get to know me, all the while he was formulating a plan for how I could best present myself and my strengths to the interviewers. I was actually pretty surprised when he gave me a "homework assignment," yet it was this preparation between meetings that allowed me to become more comfortable talking about myself, my accomplishments, and the contributions I could make to the incoming class of students. Prior to that first meeting, I was aware of the impressive number of students admitted to the program of their choice after working with Mr. Goldberg. I am pleased to be among his "success stories" and am so very grateful for his commitment to me and so many others through the years in helping each of us realize the first step in the pursuit of our professional goals. His commitment doesn't end there, as he continues to make himself available for progress updates and planning for the next phase of the journey. Mr. Goldberg is truly a generous, selfless man!

– Liam Fischer

———

Mr. Goldberg is a great role model for others. He truly takes time out of his busy schedule so that he can help the youth aspire to reach their ultimate goal of being physicians. Mr. Goldberg has a passion for what he does. He is very personable, approachable, and reliable. He helped me to get into a direct medical program. His advice and preliminary tips are so helpful that it makes you practice and study yourself before the big day. I am so grateful to have Mr. Goldberg as a role model and resource because he truly is a man who is compassionate and helpful toward others.

– Andrew M. Cardoza

———

I had the pleasure of working with Mr. Goldberg while preparing to interview for medical school. Mr. Goldberg coached me in a one-afternoon crash course, teaching me how to highlight my strengths, answer difficult questions, and discuss prior experiences in a meaningful way. He helped refine my interviewing skills so that I would be the best applicant possible and could have meaningful conversations in interviews. He was incredibly accessible and made sure to take time out of his schedule to make sure that I succeeded. I appreciate everything Mr. Goldberg did to help me matriculate into medical school, and I look forward to working with him to strengthen my residency application in the future.

– Alex Glazer

———

Mr. Goldberg is incredibly knowledgeable about medical school admissions and requirements. He is excellent at molding the perfect candidate for medical school. That being said, he does not churn out robots. Rather, he works with students to showcase aspects of our unique personalities and highlights the parts that would make us excellent candidates.

Not only is Mr. Goldberg a source of inspiration with the time and effort he puts into his students, but also inspires us to do much better. I think we've all been reminded that there is always more work to do, but Mr. Goldberg can pinpoint and improve exactly those areas that need more work.

He has helped me from the medical admission essays to the interview, and I can happily say I've been accepted into an incredibly competitive seven-year BS/MD program. I am very grateful for the time he took out of his schedule to help me, and the results truly speak for themselves.

– Katyayini Aribindi

———

The tutoring I received from Mr. Goldberg during the application process was an essential ingredient to my success in gaining admission to the Medical College at Rush University. In fact, when it was time for me to apply for my residency, I once again contacted Mr. Goldberg to consult with him on strategies to gain my ideal residency. I found Mr. Goldberg to be kind, patient, and extremely knowledgeable on the viewpoints of admissions staff. He also has a keen eye for detail which proved to be a fabulous tool for helping me to refine my interview skills and personal statement. If possible, I would suggest that all pre-med students consider utilizing his tutoring services, as well as obtaining a copy of his book for important tips on acing the medical school interview.

– Nathan Pierce

———

Thank you so much for the help you gave me both revising my personal statement and preparing for an interview! Before working with you, I had applied to medical school twice before and had never even been invited for an interview. This time not only was I invited to the earliest round of interviews, but I was admitted to the University of Illinois at the end of October. Your help and guidance were absolutely invaluable and helped me to succeed. Thank you again!

– Ryder Moses

———

Mr. Goldberg and the "Goldberg" method were extremely helpful in preparing for medical school interviews. My undergraduate grades weren't amazing, but after talking to Mr. Goldberg, we were able to highlight strengths in my application and use it efficiently during the interview process. I believe that Mr. Goldberg and his interview preparation gave me the confidence to excel during the interview, which in turn, played a crucial role in my acceptance. Thanks again, Mr. Goldberg!

– Michael O'Laughlin

———

I was referred to Ed Goldberg by my father. Mr. Goldberg had helped my two older sisters with their interviewing skills, and both were admitted to professional schools after benefitting from his aid. Mr. Goldberg had a very "tough love" attitude; he was one hundred percent willing to help me, but he wasn't going to sugar coat anything.

Had it not been for his help, I would not have been so comfortable in my final few interviews, and was accepted to Harvard School of Dental Medicine.

– Matt McShane

As a mature student, I was hesitant about my ability to compete with the large numbers of students applying for medical schools. I was certainly in the minority as an applicant and needed some help from a professional that knows the details about what medical schools are looking for. Luck was on my side when I met Mr. Goldberg, the CEO of St. Alexius Medical Center, in Hoffman Estates, Illinois. He was able to coach me on answers to key questions, my presentation, and my strengths that would tip the scales in my favor. His approach is direct, with unmistakable clarity. Prior to my coaching from Mr. Goldberg, I had applied to numerous medical schools, spending over five thousand dollars on application fees, specific prerequisites, travel to interviews, and professional testing. The result was disappointing and the wait time was aggravating. After consulting with Mr. Goldberg, I applied at my first choice medical school and was notified of my acceptance into their program within ten days. If I had known that he has the ability to know exactly what to do to get into a top notch medical school, I would have hired him two years ago and saved myself a lot of money and grief!

– Diane Roche

SO, YOU
WANT TO BE
A PHYSICIAN?

CHAPTER 15

REFERENCE RESOURCES

Exploring a Medical Career

The Association of American Medical Colleges (AAMC) has an article with several questions prospective medical students might ask themselves: Is medical career right for me? What does it take to be a doctor? What is the career of a physician like? How much do doctors make, how many hours do they work, and what is medical school like? At the time of publication, the article could be found at: https://www.aamc.org/students/considering/exploring_medical/.

Get Accepted into Medical School

About.com had an interesting article on this topic on their Health Careers page. The article provides helpful tips on how to get into medical school by suggesting that students look beyond just grades and MCAT scores in their efforts to stand out from the crowd. Prospective students can add to their chances of being accepted to medical school by showing their interest in giving back to their community through volunteer roles, leadership positions, and altruism. At the time of publication, the article could be found at:

http://healthcareers.about.com/od/educationtraining/qt/MDSchoolAccept.htm

For additional guidance on this subject, the AAMC website provides further information on how to prepare academically for medical school, how to choose the right school for undergraduate education, and how to choose the right medical school. Also discussed are topics such as when a student should apply to medical school, how students should apply, what the MCAT exam is like, and details on what medical schools look for in an applicant and how they decide which individuals to pick. At the time of publication, the article could be found at: https://www.aamc.org/students/considering/gettingin/85128/considering_gettingin.html

The Road to Becoming a Doctor

The AAMC has an extensive brochure on this subject available online. The topics covered include information on the different types of physicians, the medical education process, the length of residency for selected specialties, medical student debt, and continuing medical education. At the time of publication, the article could be found at: https://www.aamc.org/download/68806/data/road-doctor.pdf

Future Changes to the MCAT

Traci Tillman, a staff reporter for the *Yale Daily News,* summed up the future changes to the MCAT well in her article, "Future Pre-Meds Will Take New MCAT." The article discusses the four main MCAT content changes, which include the revamping of the exam's two natural science sections, the addition of an evaluation of social and behavioral sciences, and the inclusion of ethics and philosophy questions in the verbal reasoning section. The writing sample section of the test will be eliminated. At the time of publication, the article could be found at: http://www.yaledailynews.com/news/2011/apr/06/future-pre-meds-will-take-new-mcat/

Preparing for the MCAT

The AAMC provides excellent information on how students should prepare for the MCAT and suggests that students should begin their study plan a minimum of three months before their scheduled exam date. Their website provides details on the exam content, how the exam is scored, and how to select a test date. Students are also told about exam fees, testing rules, and how medical schools use the MCAT scores. At the time of publication, the article could be found at: https://www.aamc.org/students/applying/mcat/preparing/85558/study_plan.html

MCAT Scores and GPAs for Applicants and Matriculants to US Medical Schools

Students who wish to gain a better understanding of what type of grades and scores they need to get into medical school can look at the AAMC's latest research on the topic. The research shows the average MCAT scores by test section and the average GPA of medical school applicants in comparison to the same data collected on matriculants in 2011. For example, the mean total MCAT score of applicants in 2011 was 28.2, and applicants' mean GPA totals were 3.53. In comparison, the mean total MCAT score of matriculants in 2011 was 31.1, with an average mean GPA total of 3.67. At the time of publication, the research could be found at: https://www.aamc.org/download/161692/data/table18.pdf

For more information about the race and sex of applicants, acceptees, and matriculants, students can view a variety of tables outline the results of research conducted by the AAMC. One of the most complete tables, at the time of publication, could be found at: https://www.aamc.org/download/161194/data/table12.pdf

How to Get Off the Medical School Wait List

Ibrahim Busnaina published an article on October 24, 2011, on www.usnews.com, which provides examples of creative ideas on how students can make the jump from the wait list to becoming a medical school acceptee. At the time of publication, the article could be found at: http://www.usnews.com/education/blogs/medical-school-admissions-doctor/2011/10/24/how-to-get-off-the-medical-school-wait-list

The Training of Medical Students

Andis Robeznieks, a journalist for *Modern Healthcare*, wrote an interesting article on February 27, 2012, called, "New Rounds for Med Students: Revised Admissions Test and a Changing Focus for Essential Skills Will Bring a Fresh Look to Next Generation of Physicians." The article discusses the focus on new co-training programs with other caregivers and the desire for medical school students to develop good bedside manners. The article also describes how the public thinks medical schools are doing in educating new doctors, and how the new MCAT will affect students. At the time of publication, the article could be found on the Modern Healthcare website, www.modernhealthcare.com. Please note that a subscription is needed to view this article.

Medical and Dental Brigades

Participating on brigade to provide medical and dental services for those in need around the world can provide students with invaluable experience, as well as a wider global perspective. There are several groups that facilitate this type of program, but one of the most prominent organizations is Global Brigades, www.globalbrigades.org/programs.

Identifying Behaviors of Successful Medical School Students and Residents

The AAMC produced a wonderful publication in 2001 ("Identifying Behaviors of Successful Medical Students and Residents," November 2001, Vol. 1, No.4) that details the attributes that help identify students who would likely become successful physicians. Characteristics examined include skills, values, attitudes, and knowledge.

Residency

A great resource for general information on residency programs can be found on the AAMC website. The PDF publication describes the residency application process and how matching works, and it provides quality suggestions on how to ease the transition from medical school to residency. The information can be found, at the time of publication, at: https://members.aamc.org/eweb/upload/Roadmap%20to%20Residency%202ndEd.pdf

Physician Compensation

There are several articles detailing pay scales for physicians in different specialties, but the best source for information on the topic can be found on the Medical Group Management Association website: http://www.mgma.com/physcomp/

APPENDIX A

EXAMPLES OF PERSONAL STATEMENTS

Student #1:

First Example from Student #1

The best stories are those that have the most unexpected endings. Fifteen-year-old girls across the world wept when J. K. Rowling killed off their favorite headmaster, and the 2000 US Presidential election will go down in history for being decided not by our "error-proof" democracy, but by our grandparents and their sun-kissed neighbors in Florida. The surprising plot twists of both *New York Times* best sellers and everyday real lives are what make us jump out of our seats and do a Jersey Shore fist pump before all rationality can tell us to hold back. While I may not know what ending the fortune cookie gods have in store for me, I do know that I plan on making my life anything but ordinary.

I did a good job standing out right off the bat, or better yet, right out of the womb. Though having been beaten in subsequent years, I was once one of the youngest patients at Children's Memorial Hospital in Chicago to undergo dermatologic laser surgery. Being poked and prodded by medical professionals at such an early age, it's no wonder that the last thing I wanted was to become a doctor. No, I wanted to be a singer…then a dancer…then an Olympic swimmer. Scratch that, Olympic diver. After all, they got to spin in the air. But thanks to Newton and those silly laws of physics, being an international diving sensation just was not in the cards for me. I became a wandering nomad in the abyss of undetermined majors and uncertain futures called adolescence.

Then in the summer of 2009, I had the opportunity to travel to Israel with my two best friends through a program called Birthright. The trip is aimed to help young Jewish people learn about their religious and cultural identity through experience rather than narration. Like my first kiss, Israel opened my eyes to a whole new side of life. Exhilarating and welcoming, one could only laugh at the thought they had never experienced such pure chaotic happiness before. I was no longer on the outside of a closed door, wishing to understand that wet, uncoordinated initiation of love. I was finally inside the room smiling from ear to ear. I loved everything; the pushy pedestrians at the bus stop unafraid to step on your toes to get on first; the sleek oil in the Israeli cuisine, whether it is in the familiar hummus and pita or the "I don't recognize this meat" special that slipped out just as easily as it slipped in. For the first time, I loved something for myself, something out of my own conviction, rather than through my inheritance. Don't get me wrong, I love my family, but all my interests, all the major loves of my life – sports, science, Adam

Sandler movies – all of them were characteristics of my last name, rather than my first. For me, Israel was my first taste of originality, of having my own extraordinary plan. I promised myself from then on that I would pursue what made me happy, no matter the inevitable vulnerability and fear that accompanies stepping out on your own.

My junior year I went back to Israel hand-in-hand with vulnerability and fear as a part of a study abroad class through the University of Illinois with eighteen other students I didn't know. Eighteen other students who weren't Jewish, eighteen other students who had no idea what Birthright was. Therefore, when everyone was as excited as I was when we boarded the bus after our visit to Geisher Al Wadi Elementary School, I knew the pride I felt wasn't just a Jewish thing, but rather a human thing. Gesher Al Wadi is one of only four very unique schools in the State of Israel. What's so special about these schools? Well, these schools are bilingual schools. That's right – Arabic and Hebrew are spoken, and taught, in the very same classroom, beginning in kindergarten. Children from both sides of the conflict get the opportunity to learn about each other in a positive environment instead of the kind of situations you see on the news or hear on TV. When the third grade class beat the fourth grade class in a competitive soccer match, there was quite the celebration. Dr. A., the vice principal of the school, laughed as he told us, "When you ask the winners how they did it, the Jewish kids answered because their Arab friends were so good and the Arab kids answered because their Jewish friends were so good." As Dr. A. showed me, all it takes to change the world is one new idea. All it took to change my world was one new option.

My father and uncle are successful pediatricians in the suburbs of Chicago. I got the wonderful pleasure of inheriting a summer job in my father's office. My job title was Medical Assistant. As a medical assistant, you are right there in the action. You put the patient in the room, take vitals, record any problems, perform tests, and give vaccines. Pre-med friends of mine would kill for this kind of experience. For two years I was indifferent to working there. The repetition of the job was agonizing to me. Soon after starting, a robot version of me was born, merely floating through the everyday motions. Charting and giving routine shots was not interesting, and listening to crying babies definitely was not fun.

Then last summer, my uncle brought me in a room during an examination. I thought he just wanted me to help hold the child so he could continue his examination, but instead he asked me, "What do you see on the patient?" I counted all the fingers, all the toes, checked the number of limbs, and then proceeded to stare at my uncle in all seriousness and say, "A baby." He laughed and said, "Look harder." So I looked at the baby's face – two eyes, nose, and mouth – check. I just smiled and said, "A very handsome baby." Now the mom was smiling. My uncle pointed to the patient's neck. On the left side there was a massive lump. My uncle referred to it as a benign cyst. All I could muster was a half-hearted, "Cool," while figuratively hitting myself on the head.

How could I have missed such an obvious deviation from normal? When we left the room, my uncle said, "The most important thing any good doctor can do in an examination is look at the patient. By just looking you get more information than any test can give you." After that, medicine got interesting.

In the same summer, I had the pleasure of meeting one of my dad's favorite patients, Elliott. Elliott is an adolescent boy with Down syndrome. Elliott was put in a room like every other patient, but when my dad went in the room, something out of the ordinary happened. Over the intercom, my dad said, "Paging Dr. Elliott, paging Dr. Elliott, you are needed in room 2." Since we don't have a Dr. Elliott and it wasn't too busy, I joined my dad in the patient's room to see what all the noise was about. After all, I would have rather done anything than file more lab results. I watched as my dad took his stethoscope off of his neck and put it correctly on Elliott. If Elliott was going to be a doctor, he needed the proper equipment. When Elliott heard the "lubdub" of my dad's heart, the only smile bigger than Elliott's was that of his mom. My dad showed me for the first time that medicine can be fun. The relationships with the patients, the ability to help the five-year old girl with the tiara believe she is a princess for one more day, or the hug you give the modest high school grad that has come a long way from kicking the door at the sight of needles, that is where the fun is.

From my family I have learned the virtues and ideals that I hold dear, but it is from my own conviction that I have decided to pursue a career in medicine. In no other field can I find a perfect blend of exact science and creativity that so greatly matches my interests. From a few life experiences, I have found that pushing my own personal boundaries and taking a few independent steps, no matter how lonely they may seem, have proven to be the most rewarding and effective. Although I do not know where my story will end, I know that my insistence on bettering myself and my life will make one great story, full of the unexpected.

Comments:
* Another student I believe trying to be cute. I loved all of the J. K. Rowling movies, but the reference to Harry Potter is not cute, at least not to me. Some Harry Potter–loving professionals might like it, but I think the risk is too high.
* The comment about the election and "sun-kissed" neighbors in Florida is terrible. I recommend never talk about politics.
* The Jersey Shore fist pump! What academic physician on an admissions committee would not be offended?
* Why would anyone say they wanted to be anything other than a physician — a singer, a dancer, an Olympic diver — none of them are even science- or service-related.

Talking about religion is as bad as talking about politics unless it's a mission trip helping people. Please don't.

The medical experience was great and was worked into the final draft.

Second Example from Student #1

"Our job is improving the quality of life, not just delaying death. Why can't we treat death with a certain amount of humanity and dignity, and decency, and God forbid, maybe even humor? Death is not the enemy, gentlemen. If we're going to fight a disease, let's fight one of the most terrible diseases of all, indifference."

— Patch Adams

Working in my dad and uncle's pediatric office in the suburbs of Chicago over the last four summers, I have had the privilege of seeing many aspects of the medical world that other pre-med students would probably give an arm and a leg for. As a medical assistant, I do anything and everything to help my dad and uncle get through the day efficiently and effectively, whether that means running a strep test or giving well visit vaccines. Despite all my responsibilities, my favorite job, as my uncle likes to remind me, is "owwee" control coordinator and lollipop distributor. He says I am the reason why the lollipop industry will never be going into recession. I smile and say, "Good thing you don't give away iPods."

My lollipop enthusiasm probably comes from my upbringing. At a very young age, I was shown the immeasurable distance a little good deed could travel. From first grade to high school, I belonged to the Kindness Club, a group of girls dedicated to helping various causes on a monthly basis. Over the years we did everything from raising money to train a seeing eye dog to sewing over twenty blankets to donate to Project Linus, a non-profit organization whose mission is to "provide love, a sense of security, warmth, and comfort to children who are seriously ill, traumatized, or otherwise in need." If you asked me as a twelve-year old what it felt like to do these activities, I would tell you it felt good. However, not until I was older did I discover how much helping others would help me.

In the fall of 2008, I was a bright-eyed college freshman ready to embrace the best four years of my life. I would make lots of friends, do well in school, and mature into a sophisticated individual in an environment away from home. Unfortunately, I was not prepared for the stress of living a life totally dedicated to the needs of one person – myself. For the first time in my life, I was completely and totally responsible for my actions and well-being. I didn't have to coordinate dinner plans with my parents. Even scarier, I was now in charge of my own laundry, bleach and softener included. I was completely immersed in my own life and my life alone. It was in this selfish lifestyle that I became uninterested in my life, and in effect, totally miserable. I would sleep all day to avoid the indifference I felt, the kind of indifference that makes one think, "What's the point?" Once my dad caught wind of what was going on, he made me come home to see a specialist. In March 2009 during my second semester in college, I was diagnosed with an adjustment disorder heading toward depression. That day I decided it was time for me to change the way I was living. I needed to free myself of my vanity and take the focus off of myself. W. B. Yeats once wrote, "Only God, my dear, could love you for yourself alone and not your yellow hair." The same day I visited my psychologist, I walked into a local hair salon and cut off ten inches of my hair to be donated to Locks of Love. An immeasurable weight was lifted off of my shoulders, literally, and on that day I started to feel better.

Growing up as the daughter of a pediatrician and the sister of a medical school student, I was originally hesitant to put all my eggs in the "future doctor" basket because I did not want to go into the field for the wrong reason – familiarity. I wanted to pave my own way, and as such I have dabbled in some other fields of expertise, like book editing and global relations. However, despite my best efforts, something has always brought me back to medicine. In no other field can I find a perfect blend of exact science and compassion toward others that so greatly matches my passion.

In high school I had the chance to pick my own classes for the first time. Science and math always had a pull on me but the upper-level sciences, as I would reassert in college, carried a whole new level of intrigue. High school also taught me the art of prioritizing and multitasking. Being a three year varsity athlete, it wasn't always easy finding time for school, family, and friends. Despite some trying times, I was able to perform well both on the field, receiving All-Conference and All-Area recognition, as well as in the classroom, graduating with a weighted GPA of 4.52 and winning the Athletic Academic Award, given to three senior athletes with the top three GPAs.

In college I continued to explore my passion of science, specifically chemistry. In the fall of my junior year, I joined a very successful research group under the guidance and supervision of Dr. S. With the help of the team and my wonderful graduate student supervisor, Mr. O., I have learned a great deal about inorganic chemistry, its applications (medical and otherwise) and its infinite potential to help the world. I am writing a senior thesis about my two years of research in the group.

I found that at school, my freedom and independence allowed me more time for some of my hobbies. Freshman year I was elected the president of ShiAi, a philanthropic organization that consists of members from all sororities on campus. Single-handedly, I created a fundraiser for the Champaign Humane Society called "Pennies for Puppies" that was so successful it became an annual event for the organization. Sophomore year I started work on implementing the body image program into my sorority. The body image program is the first scientifically supported evidence based eating disorders prevention program designed for and with sororities. Reflections endeavors to help participants resist the ultra-thin, unrealistic ideal standard of female beauty prevalent in today's society. Self-esteem is such a huge issue for young women and a struggle very close to my heart. So when my friend in a different sorority told me about the body image program, I had to get involved. After two years of meetings, paperwork, and training, the program was finally implemented in the fall of 2009. Sophomore year was also the year I decided to try out for the women's club softball team at U of I. Freshman year I had decided to hang up my cleats after twelve years with the idea that it was time to move on. Unfortunately, my heart and my bat were not ready to give up and what followed was the best season of my life.

Comment:

* Maybe only 5 percent of all physicians would appreciate the Patch Adams reference, approximately 70 percent would disapprove, and 25 percent might not care. Why risk it?
* Keep your personal laundry at home – don't volunteer it.

Third Example from Student #1

I have known three things since an early age. I feel better about myself when I help others, particularly children; I enjoy science, particularly chemistry; and being a physician would allow me to actively help people in an area that is so important, their health.

From first grade through high school I belonged to the Kindness Club, a group of girls dedicated to helping various causes on a monthly basis. Over the years we did everything from raising money and training a seeing eye dog, to sewing more than twenty blankets to donate to Project Linus, a non-profit organization whose mission is to provide love, a sense of security, and comfort to children who are seriously ill, traumatized, or who are otherwise in need.

I graduated high school with a weighted grade point average of 4.52 out of 4.00. I played three years of varsity softball and was the MVP of the softball team and was awarded the achievement award for the athlete with the highest GPA at my school. At a very young age, I was shown the immeasurable distance that a good deed could travel.

At the U of I, I was the president of Shi Ai, which is a group that performs philanthropic activities through Champaign-Urbana and is made up of all members of the twenty sororities on campus. I created "Pennies for Puppies," a fundraiser for the local dog shelter. Because of the success of the event, it became an annual event.

I believe that many women, including myself, have struggled with their weight and all that goes along with being a "bigger girl," and I became the body image coordinator from my sorority and spent two years implementing the program.

I continued my interest in science at the University of Illinois by being a chemistry major with a minor in English and achieved a 3.7 grade point average from a possible 4.0.

I have shadowed Dr. C., a pediatric ophthalmologist, as well as Dr. M., a pediatric infectious disease physician, which was very exciting and educational, and was consistent with my goal of helping children.

I have performed, and am currently in the process of performing, research for Professor S., an extremely successful inorganic chemistry researcher and one of the reasons the University of Illinois Chemistry graduate program is in the top five of the nation. I am under the supervision of Mr. O., a graduate student, and together we are trying to create super-paramagnetic nanoparticles for drug delivery using Professor S.'s ultrasonic spray paralysis. I am writing a senior thesis from my two years of research in Dr. S.'s lab. Despite the broken glass, it's extremely rewarding because the research is aimed to better the world and help others through technology.

I believe a significant factor that has encouraged me to be a physician is the impact that working with my father and uncle as a medical assistant in their office. They are successful pediatricians in the suburbs of Chicago. As a medical assistant, you are right there in the action. You put the patient in the room, take vitals, record any problems, perform tests, and give vaccines. I can safely hold a kicking and screaming child in my sleep.

Last summer, my uncle brought me in a room during an examination. I thought he just wanted me to help hold the child so he could continue his examination. Instead he asked me, "What do you see on the patient?" I counted all the fingers, all the toes, checked the number of limbs, and proceeded to stare at my uncle with all seriousness and say, "A baby." He laughed and said, "Look harder," so I looked at the baby's face, two eyes, a nose, and mouth – check. I just smiled and said, "A very handsome baby," and now the mom was smiling. My uncle pointed to the patient's neck. On the left side there was a massive lump, and my uncle referred to it as a benign cyst. All I could muster was a half-hearted, "Ohhhh," while figuratively hitting myself on the head. How could I have missed such an obvious deviation from normal? When we left the room, Uncle Sam told me, "One of the most important functions any good doctor can do in an examination is look at the patient; just by looking you get more information than many tests can provide." After that, my interest in medicine was heightened.

I also had the pleasure of meeting one of my dad's favorite patients, Elliott, who is an adolescent boy with Down syndrome. Elliott was put in a room like every other patient, but when dad went into the room something out of the ordinary happened. Over the intercom, my dad said, "Paging Doctor Elliott – paging Doctor Elliott – you are needed in Room 2." Since we don't have a Doctor Elliott and it wasn't too busy, I joined my dad in the patient's room to see what all the noise was about. I watched as my dad took his stethoscope off his neck and put it directly on Elliott. If Elliott was going to be a doctor he needed the proper equipment. When Elliott heard the "lubdub" of my dad's heart, the only smile bigger than Elliott's was that of his mother. My dad showed medicine could be fun for the patient and help to engage them in working together in ensuring or improving their health. The relationships with the patients, the ability to help the five-year old girl with a tiara believe she is a princess for one more day, or receive a hug from the modest high school grad that has come a long way from kicking the door at the sight of needles is where the personal reward comes. This is what motivates and excites me.

I recognize that medicine is a profession that requires vigorous attainment of knowledge and expertise. From my family, I have learned the virtues and ideals that I hold dear, but it is through my own conviction that I decided to pursue a career in medicine. In no other field can I find a perfect blend of exact science and compassion toward others that so greatly matches my passion.

One of my favorite jobs, as my uncle likes to remind me, is "owwee" control coordinator and lollipop distributor. I believe my lollipop enthusiasm combined with a caring empathic attitude demonstrates full circle the immeasurable distance a good deed can travel.

I believe medicine is the greatest medium in which people can help others. Whether it is showing a Down syndrome child how to use a stethoscope so they wouldn't be afraid of it, to the delight of the patient and his smiling mother, to the confidence of a ten-year old blossom when her eye doctor tells her how beautiful she looks in her new glasses. I want to be a physician, not only because I want to help people but because I want to engage with people and be touched by their lives as I can hopefully touch theirs. I want to be a physician who treats the human condition, not just the illness. I want to bring warmth, compassion, and perhaps laughter to help gain the patient's trust. If I have the honor of receiving an invitation to your medical school, I know I will carry with me the lessons of pursuing greatness through compassion, warmth and hard work. After all, sometimes all it takes is a lollipop, a little magic and warmth.

Comment: Same student, different draft. I loved the office experience and importance of humanness. I would have left off some of the personal and extracurricular activities not relevant to medical school.

Fourth Example from Student #1

From first grade through high school I belonged to the Kindness Club, a girls' volunteer group dedicated to helping various causes on a monthly basis. We did everything from raising money to train a seeing-eye dog, to sewing blankets for donations aimed at helping seriously ill or traumatized children. My involvement in the Kindness Club deeply engrained a passion for giving within me, and it was not until I formalized my decision to become a doctor that I realized the true value of these experiences in my youth.

Upon reaching high school, I was thrilled to finally choose my courses. Science and math had always piqued my interest so I challenged myself in Advanced Placement sciences, which heightened my level of intrigue. While the coursework kept me busy, I was not hesitant to explore other talents and interests. Varsity athletics filled my schedule for three years and I was forced to develop a way to prioritize and allow time to develop socially. Admittedly, difficulties arose but I routinely found solace in the notion that my hard work would one day allow me to pursue my passion of giving. With this strengthened determination I performed well in athletics, receiving All-Conference and All-Area recognition, as well as in the classroom, graduating with a weighted GPA of 4.52 and winning the Athletic Academic Award, which was given to only three senior athletes with the top GPAs.

Entering college, I continued exploring science, specifically chemistry. In my junior year I joined Dr. S. in his student research group. Along with the research team, I have had the unique opportunity to apply my knowledge of inorganic chemistry in a real research environment. Because of this experience I have become fascinated with its applications (medical and otherwise), as well as its great potential to better our world.

Over the past three summers I have worked in my father and uncle's pediatric office in the suburbs of Chicago. As a medical assistant, I contribute wherever Dad or Uncle Sam need me to, from performing strep tests to administering well visit vaccines. While developing an understanding of the logistics had been interesting, it is without a doubt my response to witnessing patient interactions that proves medicine is the right path for me.

One of my dad's patients, an adolescent boy, Elliott, with Down syndrome, made a memorable visit my first summer. The boy was assigned to a room like every other patient, but when Dad entered the room, something out of the ordinary happened. Over the intercom I heard my father's voice, "Paging Doctor Elliott – paging Doctor Elliott – you are needed in Room 2." Out of pure curiosity I joined my dad in the patient's room. My eyes were fixated as he placed his stethoscope around Elliott's neck. Surely, if Elliott was going to be the doctor he needed the proper equipment. When Elliott heard the "lubdub" of my dad's heart I quickly noticed that the only smile in that room bigger than Elliott's was that of his mother.

In that moment my dad showed me that medicine could bring joy to the patient, something I rarely realized as a serious science student. More importantly, I saw that as a doctor, engaging patients is not simply for fun – it is crucial. Building strong patient/doctor relationships, convincing the five-year-old girl with a tiara that she is a princess, or hugging the mature high school graduate that once sat kicking the door in fear of needles brings an indescribable reward. These memories are my motivation.

I recognize that medicine is a profession that requires vigorous attainment of knowledge and expertise. From my family I have learned the necessity of this profession, but it is through my own conviction that I have decided to pursue a career in medicine. Medicine, I believe, is the greatest medium in which kindness is achieved. My childhood experiences in the Kindness Club leap to the surface of my mind because the intense feelings of gratification, pride, and confidence involved with the impact of giving has driven me to this point.

I want to be a doctor not only because I am confident in my knowledge of science, but because I want to engage people and be touched by their lives – as I can hopefully touch theirs. I want to be a physician who treats the human condition, not just the illness. Along with precision I will bring warmth, compassion, and perhaps laughter to the everyday patient/doctor interactions.

I thank you for considering my application, and if I have the honor of receiving an invitation to your medical school I will carry with me the lesson of pursuing greatness through passion, dedication and hard work.

Comment: *Good discussion of the human experience of working with patients. Accepted into the medical school of her choice. This woman had the grades, MCAT score, service and poise to get in. Why risk it all with an out there, too creative, too funny personal statement?*

—

Student #2

I decided to become a physician later than most. This was not due to a lack of exposure; my mother is a pediatric anesthesiologist. I was born while she was in medical school and my sister while she was in residency. With my dad working around the country, we were raised during those early years mostly by her parents. Nevertheless, I still admire my mom more than any woman I know. She works harder than I can possibly imagine, and her stories of interesting patients, close saves, and terrible losses were inspiring. But her long hours and time spent away from home always rankled, as did her bitter, openly stated regret at not being there as her children grew up. Thus, in high school, I focused more on math and physics, and tried to avoid biology as much as possible. Once I got to college, I thought my career was set. I liked machines, outer space, and things that go boom – rocket science it was.

I also felt that I owed something back to the society that had given me so much while I was growing up, compared to what I saw during family trips to India. The grinding poverty was evident while driving along dusty roads to visit my father's birth town: cripples on every street corner and rail-thin children and families living under threat from zealots of all stripes. I decided to join Air Force ROTC, and pay back some of the debt that I owed to my country for giving me a childhood free from danger and hunger.

Life had different plans. I joined MIT's student-run ambulance service on a lark; driving with lights and sirens screaming through Boston seemed like a fun thing to do. And indeed it was, but not for the reason I was expecting. By day, I would sit in class, taking notes, solving equations. But nights and weekends, my job went from adding and subtracting numbers to taking care of people. To the considerable relief of my supervisors, I rapidly lost the desire to hit sixty mph going against traffic on a one-way street, responding to a patient with an isolated ankle injury. But I am still deeply honored that patients of all ages, races, and sexes would respect and trust me, then a nineteen-year-old college student, to take care of them.

The summer after freshman year, due to AFROTC's training requirements, I looked for a flexible job that would allow me to leave in the middle to go to an airbase in Alaska. My own PCP had an opening and gave me a shot. She had recently made the transition to EMR and needed someone to enter patient data. As I was an EMT, she also had me take vitals, HPIs, AMPLE history, and notes in the room while she talked to the patient, and assist her in her minor office procedures. Needless to say, holding the basin while she performed ear irrigations and testing urine samples wasn't the most glamorous stuff. But the patients' smiles and heartfelt thank yous after we had treated them as best we could were more uplifting than I could have imagined. Lengthening and improving other people's lives was my job – it was one of the most rewarding things I had ever done.

Two events finally settled me on medicine. First, I completed an internship at MIT Lincoln Laboratories doing aerospace software design for national defense. My colleagues were smart and great to work with, and the work was challenging and interesting. But while my work engaged my intellectual capacities, it didn't feel that meaningful. Aerospace engineering as a whole up to this point had been fun. I still remember the fierce rush of pride as the RC plane my team designed and built flew for the first time. (Though it was soon mitigated by horror as the six-foot foam wing broke in half upon landing, necessitating frantic resuscitation attempts as the plane was due for a grade in forty-eight hours.) But while engineering was fun, it was never as fulfilling as my medical experiences.

Soon after, I found out that my mother had been diagnosed with lupus. I understood little about the disease, but I did know the prognosis included flares and organ failure. With hospital stays on the horizon, I couldn't commission into the air force and be unable to visit her should she suffer from flares in the future; the nearest air force base is five hundred miles away from home. I made the painful decision to withdraw from AFROTC. Furthermore, her illness made me realize even more how much relief and joy doctors bring not only to their patients, but to their patients' loved ones as well. I made the decision to start the long road to becoming a physician.

Switching courses has been neither fun nor easy, as I find myself competing with freshmen and sophomores and taking summer courses to complete both my aerospace degree and pre-medical requirements on time. I understand all too well the personal sacrifices that I am making and that I am forcing my future family to make. But I've realized that my engineering background is still useful in designing and evaluating both medical devices and organizations, as well as developing technology to better deliver care. And more than anything, I am looking forward to the day I will have patients of my own. While I am apprehensive of the great responsibility, I know the payoff, their smiling faces, is well worth the cost.

Comment: *I suggested several changes, only a few of which were accepted by the student. I didn't like the reference to the ambulance service as a "lark" and "seems like fun." I also felt having many career changes was not beneficial. All that being said, a 38 on the MCAT spoke for itself.*

Student #3

In its mission statement, the UIC Honors College is described as a community of scholars whose goal is to enrich the educational experience of undergraduates and allow faculty and students of all disciplines to interact in teaching, learning and research. What scholarly attributes do you bring to this community and what do you expect in return?

As I sat listening to the University of Illinois Chicago's Honors College presentation one chilly November morning, I envisioned myself as a student on campus. I was impressed by the abundance and variance of research opportunities and found myself avidly taking notes about the prospects of engaging in honors coursework and participating in student organizations that I knew would help enrich my college education. I feel that my scholarly credentials qualify me for consideration into the UIC honors track. Not only do I have the academic tenacity needed to take on such a stimulating curriculum, the experiences I have been able to garner for my past seventeen years of existence have allowed me to become an open-minded, creative, and compassionate leader, ready to tackle the challenges of the academic world.

My strongest and perhaps most utilized trait is my sense of open-mindedness. Because my mother is an employee of United Airlines, I have been fortunate enough to journey to six of the seven world continents. My many sojourns have allowed me to witness how others across the globe spend their days, and have also given me the opportunity to respect the various cultural and social differences that set us apart. One instance that particularly stands out in my mind is my first exposure of poverty, which occurred while I was in India. Actually walking among these individuals and witnessing their stark living conditions increased my awareness of social disparity on both a local and global level. I carry this awareness into my personal life at home as I try to empathize with my fellow classmates and teachers. This trait especially helps me with the leadership roles that I hold, both in my school and community, as it gives me greater ability to understand others' wants and needs. This trait will hopefully carry over at UIC and allow me to accept cultural and social differences that I may encounter in the university's highly diverse student body. I also envision that this trait will help me in my future career. As a potential doctor, my open-mindedness will allow me to relate and empathize with my patients.

The long hours I put into my school newspaper as presiding editor-in-chief, coupled with the speeches I regularly deliver as speech captain, exemplify my sense of creativity. In both activities I not only had to learn how to effectively motivate a group to perform at their best, I also learned the importance of thinking "out of the box" and reasoning with others' viewpoints in comparison to my own. To me, the prospect of being able to present information in a manner that I feel will captivate the minds of a 2,500-member student body excites me and pushes me to find innovative means to do so. At UIC, I plan to take advantage of this passion by writing for one of the student-organized honor journals, such as *JPHAS* or *Ampersand*. I want to be able to touch the minds of my fellow students, as well as the surrounding community in a useful manner, and feel that these outlets would help me do so.

I will bring this sense of creativity to UIC through my literary activities and also through my experience as a choreographer for the Indian Dance Academy, which I have been a part of for the past nine years. Dancing is my most valued extracurricular activity, and I am extremely thankful for having been given the opportunity to explore my roots, as well as the cultural practices of my Hindu ancestors. Through my experiences with dance, I participated in a variety of cultural showcases, talent competitions, and was even given the opportunity to dance at the

India's Independence Day Parade in Chicago for the past two years, as well as in the Museum of Science and Industry's Holidays around the World Showcase. More importantly, however, I danced for various social causes, such as cancer awareness and global poverty benefits. Through these events I garnered a sense of compassion for worldly affairs and learned how to incorporate my hobbies in order to make a greater impact on my community as a whole. At UIC, I hope to use my talents toward a similar cause, perhaps organizing a cultural charity event that would benefit both the campus community and a larger aspect of society.

The only thing I ask in return from the UIC campus and faculty is to provide me with a stimulating environment that will allow me to continue developing my talents and explore different aspects of my academic and professional interests. As an aspiring doctor, I feel that the GPPA program will allow me to gain unmatched experience within the medical field. The vast patient demographics and medical situations that await me at the Illinois Medical District cannot be found with any other institution, which is why I will gain more quality experience as a student here. I am confident that UIC will allow me to reach my professional ambition in a successful manner.

Comment: I suggested to the student that there was not enough science and too much newspaper and dance. Outside interests are fine, but they should not detract from the core of science classes. The student rejected my suggestions.

—

First Example from Student #4

I have always been fascinated by everything scientific, especially the function and complexity of living things. A strong sense of curiosity defined by a desire to understand constantly encourages me to learn more and is one reason I want to pursue a career in medicine. I have always been interested by the intricacies of systems and pathways within the human physiology, and the prospect of being able to interact with and repair these systems greatly excites me. The challenge of being able to directly affect and work to heal the human body is one that I dream of mastering; however, the opportunity to build personal connections by helping people is the primary reason I am interested in medicine.

In addition to a love of learning and excitement about medicine, my personality and general demeanor will also help me to be a compassionate physician. First, I excel when challenged and have strong problem-solving skills. My experiences while living in Japan were a true test of my abilities. When I first arrived, I had only a basic knowledge of the language. Even though I continued my studies, the challenges of integrating into such a different culture truly tested me. The Japanese language has thousands of Kanji characters, making common tasks like grocery shopping difficult. Every day was a new adventure, and I thrived knowing that everything around me would yield new challenges that needed to be understood and solved. My time in Japan also helped me to understand how focused I am and how I always strive to exceed expectations through hard work and perseverance. By the end of my stay, I was able to interact with Japanese people and form lasting friendships.

After returning, I carried these invaluable experiences with me as I continued my academic pursuits. Ever enthusiastic about science and the acquisition of knowledge, my fascination was constantly stoked by the experiences I had working with a cardiologist. By observing and learning tests and techniques commonly used to diagnose ailments, as well as how these medical problems are addressed, my desire to become a doctor was heightened. I understand and appreciate the level of skill and dedication required to become a physician. I believe my enthusiasm, determination, general caring, and accessible nature will help me to learn and embody these ideals.

Comment: I suggested mentioning more facts, GPA, and the MCAT. There was no research or experience to draw from.

Second Example from Student #4

I have always been fascinated by everything scientific, especially the function and complexity of living things. A strong sense of curiosity, defined by a desire to understand, constantly encourages me to learn more and is one reason I want to pursue a career in medicine. I have always been interested by the intricacies of systems and pathways within the human physiology, and the prospect of being able to interact with and repair these systems greatly excites me. The challenge of being able to directly affect and work to heal the human body is one that I dream of mastering; however, the opportunity to build personal connections by helping people is the primary reason I am interested in medicine.

In addition to a love of learning and excitement about medicine, my personality and general demeanor will also help me to be a compassionate physician. First, I excel when challenged and have strong problem-solving skills. My experiences while living in Japan were a true test of my abilities. When I first arrived, I had only a basic knowledge of the language. Even though I continued my studies, the challenges of integrating into such a different culture truly tested me. The Japanese language has thousands of Kanji characters, making common tasks like grocery shopping difficult. Every day was a new adventure, and I thrived knowing that everything around me would yield new challenges that needed to be understood and solved. My time in Japan also helped me to understand how focused I am and how I always strive to exceed expectations through hard work and perseverance. By the end of my stay I was able to interact with Japanese people and form lasting friendships.

After returning, I carried these invaluable experiences with me as I continued my academic pursuits. Ever enthusiastic about science and the acquisition of knowledge, my fascination was constantly stoked by the experiences I had working with a cardiologist. Since graduating from college, I am pursuing a master's degree in biotechnology and chemical sciences. During the 2011 spring semester, I participated in a medical internship that involved shadowing doctors in a variety of specialties every week.

By observing and learning tests and techniques commonly used to diagnose ailments, as well as how these medical problems are addressed, my desire to become a doctor was heightened. I understand and appreciate the level of skill and dedication required to become a physician. I believe my enthusiasm, determination, general caring and accessible nature will help me to learn and embody these ideals.

Comment: Better, but still lacking additional info, GPA, and the MCAT.

— —

First Example from Student #5

I aspired to be a physician after coming to the realization that not everyone can be the Pink Time Force (Power) Ranger. By the time I graduated from college, I had extensive knowledge of gas chromatography/mass spectrometry and how to conduct organic synthesis via microwave radiation. During my years in college, I had gained a strong passion for biomedical research; participating in research was relaxing for me. I liked it immediately. My first day in the lab, I decided that research was going to be one of my preferred extracurricular activities while in college. Engaging in research strengthened my cognitive and leadership skills, while enhancing my confidence in performing presentations. In addition to my coursework and research, I was the president of Chemistry Society for two years, during which time the organization participated in numerous academic and social activities. I also had the opportunity to travel and present my research at symposiums and national meetings organized by the American Chemical Society, allowing me the opportunity to meet renowned chemists from across the nation. While my window for having a future in research was wide open, I continued to be a determined aspiring physician.

With a solid academic background after graduation I decided to focus on expanding my healthcare experience. I was employed by PhysAssist Scribes, Inc., and in my first few months I saw multiple traumas from motor vehicle collisions, myocardial infarctions, appendicitis and small bowel obstructions, as well as many other emergency cases, and observed physicians making clinical decisions. Furthermore, I learned how to properly document medical records and became experienced using various electronic medical record systems. The greatest joy was when I was promoted to be a certified trainer scribe followed by the position of a lead trainer and started traveling to cities around the nation to train.

By the time I was a lead trainer, I had become an expert in my workforce. I had increased medical understanding, the communicator between physician and patient, and developed a strong sense of leadership and improved my communication skills. I engage with physicians on a daily basis and have started many scribe programs in various cities in the Midwest. Starting a program involves working with corporate, physician groups and the hospitals on successfully carrying out contracts, while initiating and stabilizing a productive program. The programs I have worked on have expanded after implementation, allowing me to have multiple facilities under my wing at any given time. My work has become such an integral part of my life that, similar to research, going to the hospital and doing clinical shifts and holding classroom trainings for the new scribes has been very fulfilling. This is primarily because my employment has allowed me the opportunity to travel, work with emergency physicians in different facilities, and gain insight into the practice of medicine while ensuring me of my career interest in the field of medicine.

My time traveling has allowed me to think about what inspires me to be a physician. I learned that research demands determination, dedication, courage, and strength, which are some of the defining characteristics of an ideal physician. Research interested and challenged me. By working on drug synthesis projects, I understood more about how research scientists are able to make important breakthroughs. The research and clinical aspects of medicine work in unison, while ensuring that both combined are carried out in the best interest of the patient. My experience as a scribe in the healthcare field has strengthened my initial intent to be a physician because in physicians I see the empathy and compassion I desire in my career. During each shift I think to myself…this is the reason I want to be a doctor. I want to engage with patients and problem-solve to help them through their crises. I want to be in an environment where I will be challenged constantly for the benefit of others.

Comment: *Reference to Power Rangers not a good idea. I think the student thought he was trying to be cute. Not cute — to me at least.*

Second Example from Student #5

As a high school senior, I was accepted into the Health Professions Recruitment and Exposure Program at the University of Texas-Southwestern Medical School, which exposed young students to the possibility of a career in healthcare. From anatomy to microbiology, we learned to explore the human body through the lens of science. The more I learned, the more I became fascinated. Every day was a new adventure in this program. We experienced a simulated childbirth, substituting red Kool-Aid for blood; we watched videos on how the circulatory system worked; and we read about how cells engineered energy from oxygen and glucose (brilliant!). In my final days of high school, I was certain I had to explore science and medicine during my college years.

In college, I took part in a myriad of activities, from the Indian-Pakistani Student Association to election as a residential senator in student government, all of which helped me begin developing leadership skills I would appreciate years down the line. I was accepted into the biomedical research support program, where I worked under an organic chemist, assisting in the synthesis of bisamidoximes, a chemical being explored as an anti-cancer agent. As I learned how to conduct scientific research, write grant proposals and share findings with my peers, I began to appreciate the role of research in medicine. Soon, biomedical research began evolving into an important element of my future career.

Engaging in research challenged me to ask the right questions and develop a plan to get answers. It strengthened my cognitive skills, and helped me build confidence in presenting information to colleagues. With my early successes in bench research, I was offered an opportunity to complete an accelerated master's degree in chemistry at Southern Methodist University. During this time, I kept a strong commitment to community service beyond the bench, serving as president of the Chemistry Society for two years. As president, I took initiative to mentor our members and find opportunities to improve the campus environment through talks and educational activities about chemistry (our work culminated in our organization being formally recognized by the American Chemical Society). I also had the opportunity to travel and present my research at symposiums and national meetings organized by the American Chemical Society, allowing me the chance to meet and learn from renowned chemists from across the nation. By the time I graduated, I was proficient with gas chromatography/mass spectrometry and knew how to conduct organic synthesis experiments via microwave radiation. I began to see that it took more than bench acumen to be a great researcher; it also took leadership, courage, empathy, curiosity, strength, and determination.

However, I still thirsted for a more direct, person-to-person service component to my career that research alone could not offer. I turned my focus to health care and applied for a position as a medical scribe in the emergency room with PhysAssist Scribes, Inc. My job was to work alongside emergency physicians to help them document patient medical charts. This experience gave me a fascinating and intimate window into patient care, which motivated me to be the best scribe I could be. Soon I was promoted to be a certified trainer scribe and then to the position of a lead trainer, which led me to cities around the United States to train scribes for work in emergency rooms.

To date, I have worked in over eleven different emergency departments, with more than eighty physicians. Every day poses new challenges for the doctors and, by proxy, the scribes, in figuring out how to streamline high-quality care. I have seen a range of pathology from common colds to multi-system trauma, and watched physicians, nurses, and ancillary staff work together to help people surmount the gravest of illnesses. I appreciated that, as with research, it took strength, courage, curiosity, empathy, leadership, and determination to be a great physician. The experience inspired me to pursue a career as a physician, from my foundation as a chemist and student leader.

In the past months, my experience as a scribe made me certain that I want to participate directly in patient care, though I still hold a strong allegiance to my research career. Physicians serve their communities directly by helping the sick improve the quality of their lives through diagnosis and treatment, but they can also serve their communities by moving medicine forward through scientific inquiry. Moving forward, I want to be part of a medical school community that will train me to be a stellar clinician. With a strong undergraduate medical education, I hope one day to leverage my leadership potential to help my patients both at the bedside and from behind the bench.

Comment: *Applying a year after initially being turned down for med school of choice, this student was subsequently accepted.*

Student #6

I want to pursue a career in medicine because I want to be able to answer the calls for help from the people who need attention, but do not receive as much as they need. I have always enjoyed and excelled in science and mathematics. In my junior year of high school, I began working as an aide at the dementia unit of a rehabilitation facility. Every single time I volunteered, I encountered restless residents who begged for more attention but did not receive enough. I felt they didn't receive what they needed because of their physical weakness and inability to communicate effectively. It was as if they were already dead to many. When I would look into their eyes I would see restless residents who were anything but dead. They were as alive with life as any of us – they just needed the correct attention and sympathy to answer their cries for help. Hopefully, new medications will be developed to provide further advances in the care of dementia patients. Medicine knows no bounds, and that is something that captivates me. The dementia was not limited by the color of their skin or the histories of their heritage; there were Americans, Asians, African-Americans, and Russians at the rehabilitation facility, all needing more help. I want to work to answer the call of all of these people, no matter their physical and mental orientation. The potential to help people of all kinds is the concept that motivates me to pursue a career in medicine. I hope that I will possess the ability to extend meaningful life for patients.

Comment: *Demonstrates the desire to help others.*

—

Student #7

I initiated my college education in the College of Engineering at Bradley University as a construction major. I realized that the complexities and intricacies of building any structure require a basic foundation involving many trades. While attending school and learning about construction, I started to develop an interest in the basic sciences, so I began enrolling in related courses.

I have also had the opportunity to spend time with my father, who has been a physician for twenty-five years and has exposed me to his practice and daily routine in the field of medicine. I found that my father's practice in medicine was far more enriching than construction because it not only included applications of higher learning and education, but also requires skills in personal communication with both patients and colleagues. In addition, caring for people provides more challenges and opportunities to utilize problem-solving skills, motor skills, and taking the most extreme responsibility in life by caring for another individual.

I believe that attending Bradley University in the School of Engineering has provided a building block for my educational advancement. In order to transition myself into a career in medicine, I recognized the need to expand my knowledge base in an assortment of science courses. I therefore enrolled at the University of Illinois to complete the required sciences for the medical prerequisites. Additionally, I have taken an EMT course, which provided me with some clinical experience and will better prepare me for a career in medicine. During that course, I learned the basics of emergency medical response. I also was able to work in emergency rooms, assisting the physicians in caring for patients. This not only provided a valuable learning opportunity, it has heightened my desire to pursue a career in medicine.

The next step in accomplishing my ultimate goal of becoming a physician is to further enhance my knowledge to better prepare myself for medical school. The program at Rush University will provide a solid education in the field of biotechnology and is designed to prepare future medical students for the challenge of medical school. I would appreciate you giving me the opportunity to attend your university so I can contribute to the classroom experience and complete my education and career goals.

Comment: Touches many bases, and demonstrates a solid foundation.

Student #8

I have been preparing myself academically for my future as a physician. As a physics major with interest in health care, I have been taking courses over a very wide range of subjects. I made it my goal to try to expand my scientific knowledge as much as I could. Not only have I been taking classes to fulfill requirements for my physics major, but I have also been taking classes in the biology and chemistry departments to help me prepare for my career in health care.

While these classes have been teaching me about how the human body works and develops, I have been gaining strong insight into critical thinking in completely different fields of study, such as math and physics. My studies in these subjects have given me the background to solve and analyze problems from a completely different point of view and will provide a broader spectrum of techniques and strategies to apply when approaching a problem.

As a physics major, I have been rewarded by taking classes with very strong problem solving and critical thinking backgrounds. This is one of the most important qualities/traits of a medical professional. I believe thinking critically and solving problems utilizing different strategies and techniques is a crucial element for a successful physician. My physics classes are very heavily based with problem-solving strategies and mathematical techniques that will allow me to better analyze a patient problem that I may encounter.

One experience that has had a lasting impact on my life was a mission trip I took with my family to Pivra, Peru. During this trip, we delivered food to needy families and helped build shelters in the urban area of Peru. This experience helped open my eyes to the poverty and poor conditions and minimal health care that some people live through. The memory of these struggling people has given me the incentive and courage to do whatever I can to help people as much as I can. I believe a career in medicine will provide me with the opportunities to help and promote a healthy living for others. This experience not only has shaped my desire to be a physician, but also sparked my study of Spanish, which is my minor, and in which I am conversant. I would hope to one day provide primary care to Spanish-speaking people.

I wish to become a physician in order to help people in the best way that I can. Making a difference in peoples' lives is what motivates me. Providing people with healthcare is an invaluable benefit. As a physician, I will be able to take advantage of my abilities to solve problems critically in order to provide patients with the best possible health care available.

Comment: *Good explanation as to how a background in physics can apply to medicine and caring for others.*

Student #9

Emergency Medical Services brought a patient into the St. Alexius Medical Center emergency room at 1:30 p.m. on a Thursday in May. The forty-five-year-old man recently underwent brain surgery and was suffering from post-operative seizures. Prior to his trip to the ER, doctors had been unable to control the symptoms through standard protocols, and the patient and his family was increasingly terrified with each seizure.

In the ER I witnessed one such seizure while working as a medical scribe for his emergency room physician, Dr. F. I began working as a medical scribe a few months ago, and this was one of many difficult and complex cases that I witnessed. This case was also the most personally inspirational.

The patient was quickly stabilized by the ER team, led by Dr. F., and he could have been admitted to the hospital or sent home. Dr. F. had fulfilled his basic responsibilities of stabilizing the incoming patient, making sure that he was "out of the woods" in the immediate sense. However, Dr. F. did not allow fatigue and multiple additional responsibilities to deter him from further assessing the patient and the situation. He ordered a CT scan of the chest, which is not standard protocol in this case, which showed multiple bilateral pulmonary embolisms. Had he either admitted or discharged this patient after following standard ER protocols, this man could have died at any moment. Dr. F.'s decision to order an additional test very likely saved the patient's life. This case showed me how education and training, combined with commitment and compassion, can be the difference between life and death.

As a student at the University of Michigan, I knew that I wanted to be a doctor. I learned a great deal in the classroom and as a volunteer at the Ann Arbor Veteran's Hospital. I have taken the last year to learn more about medicine and myself. I loved the training program that I took to get my emergency medical technician certification. I have learned a great deal about some of the unpleasant realities of the American healthcare system by becoming a volunteer at Community Health Clinic, a free clinic for the uninsured in Chicago. I admired the all-volunteer medical staff at the clinic. In May I was fortunate to land a position as a medical scribe at the St. Alexius Medical Center ER in suburban Chicago. Three weeks ago I was promoted to chief medical scribe. I love going to work every day (even at night).

As a volunteer at the free health clinic and working in an ER, my eyes have been opened to the many Americans that live without proper health care because they lack health insurance and, for a variety of reasons, how difficult it can be for them to maintain good health. I have seen patients walk into the Community Health Clinic and walk out feeling better because of the "care" in health care. I have seen the same thing in the emergency room at St. Alexius Medical Center. Even the small amount of time that the volunteer physicians dedicate to the patients each week makes an enormous difference.

Both these Community Health Clinic physicians and Dr. F. have shown me the compassion and dedication it takes to truly help people. I look forward to following their example and providing both the health and the care in health care. This has been a rewarding journey and I feel ready to enter medical school. I want to be a physician so I can help people feel better, live better, and live longer.

Comment: Excellent demonstration of experience as an emergency room scribe.

—

Student #10

The last Saturday of every month was the day I most dreaded. It was the day of my public recital at a local nursing home. As a beginning pianist, I would nervously walk to the piano and wonder if I had practiced enough. After finishing my piece, I would exhale a sigh of relief, finally able to slide off the bench to take a bow. This was the moment when I came face-to-face with my audience, a room full of nursing home residents seated in wheel chairs, clapping more vigorously and smiling more brightly than expected. I was surprised that my beginner's piece would command such enthusiasm. During those times, I realized my performance had personally enlivened the residents' spirits and helped them momentarily forget their physical discomfort, loneliness, or weakened wellness. My piece was a small contribution toward uplifting the residents and offering them a caring distraction. This early experience inspired me to wonder how I could better help people on an individual basis with more of my talents and efforts beyond a mere beginners' piano piece.

My inspiration to pursue medicine may have begun with these recitals but became further developed when I was introduced to a muscular dystrophy patient. "Steven" was twenty-one years old, my age, and the disease had progressed to an advanced level. He was bedridden, extremely thin, and dependent on others for even the most basic of functions. I was struck by how this disease had taken away his ability to control his life in the simplest ways, drastically changing its conditions and outcomes. If Steven had not inherited muscular dystrophy, he would be able to stand, enjoy summer athletics, and prepare for a future career, just like I had. His family was very positive and attentive to his desires. They took every opportunity to empower Steven and give him some measure of quality in life. However, outside the room, they acted differently from the smiles, optimism, and strength I witnessed within. I can never forget the image of his family holding one another in the hallway and crying as silently as they could. As I watched, I desired to know exactly how to help Steven in order to brighten this family and give them the happiness they deserved. But, I did not know what to do or say, and I felt absolutely powerless.

I observed the physician console the family members. It was apparent he had developed personal relationships with each person. As a counselor, educator, confidant, and physician, he was able to help the family precisely in the way I wanted to but was unable. He was treating Steven's condition medically, and more importantly, he was making every effort to treat the whole family's spirit. Watching their tears and anguish subside fueled my desire to have a direct role in bettering the health and lives of patients and families, just as this physician was doing. It would be an honor to be responsible for assisting a whole family and offering them support, hope, and compassion.

The memory of Steven's story is unforgettable. When learning about the molecular and genetic mechanism of muscular dystrophy, I am reminded of Steven. He has given me a connection to the disorder and the realization that my coursework offers knowledge beyond my personal fulfillment. By developing a strong science foundation, I would improve my ability to educate and treat future patients, but my interactions with Steven, the nursing home residents, and other patients have added a further dimension to my pursuit of medicine. They have rooted my academic interests in the passion to learn on behalf of future patients and their families.

Once a young child seeking to play my best on a recital piece, I am now a young adult similarly inclined to make a difference in the lives of others. The relief I felt in this accomplishment as a child has been replaced by a desire to contribute to more far-reaching consequences, touching the health and welfare of a family. Knowing the potential a recital has to provide solace for a stranger, I am inspired to utilize my perseverance and dedication to quality in the field of medicine. My experiences have given me an intense desire to impact people's lives by utilizing my education, talents, and abilities. Having learned the deeper dimensions of infirmity and humanity, I can think of no greater service than that provided by a physician.

Comment: *Very good personal experiences in wanting to help others.*

APPENDIX B

AN EXAMPLE OF A REVISED PERSONAL STATEMENT

My unrelenting drive to become a physician has been ~~drastically~~ inspired by a vast array of people, experiences, and passions. Since I was very young, my parents have instilled in me a sense of awe and wonder at the incredible beauty and complexity of the human body. Their unyielding love for the human body and helping others not only drove them to become incredible physicians, but critically influenced the way they raised me. Growing up hearing my father enthusiastically speak about a rare blood disorder or hearing my mother talking about Crohn's disease was a very normal thing. This full absorption into a world dominated by scientific reasoning and clinical passion has inspired the way that I perceive the world, and has laid a solid foundation for what I hope to do for the rest of my life. My ~~premature~~ love for knowing how systems work at a fundamental level in biology, chemistry, and physics was enough for me to decide to embark on a scientific journey in college.

As I began my classes at Boston University, I was challenged by the increased complexity of my classes and ~~overwhelming~~ workload. My first year at Boston University cast doubts on whether I would be able to perform what I most loved. It was a very frustrating time that made me more resilient and more determined to study longer hours, complete supplemental coursework, and reach out to my professors when I did not understand concepts. It was not until the summer after freshman year that I had my first calling and inspiration to become a physician.

During the summer going into sophomore year, I attended an annual picnic at my father's oncology office. It was a hot, humid summer day at a large recreational field and many families of the people who worked at the office were there. As I was eating and talking to my coworker, I noticed that she started to slur her words and stopped making any sense. At first I thought she just confused her words and ~~I joked with her,~~ asked what she meant by what she had just said. As a few seconds proceeded, I was immediately alerted that she was unable to speak and became unresponsive. In an instant of ~~intense~~ fear for my coworker's health, I immediately sprinted across the field to get the attention of my father and his coworkers and told them what had just happened. It was their reaction to my crucial information that established my drive to become a physician, and my belief that it was my destiny. As they called for paramedics, they immediately knew to check for vitals, positioned her legs upward, and performed several physiological tests. The ability of these physicians to immediately respond at this critical stage and recognize what physiological systems might be impacted and acting accordingly to potentially save the girl's life made me realize what I wanted to do with my ~~intense~~ passion for science – it was ~~my fate~~ to become a physician.

As I continued with the rest of my college career as a biology and psychology major, I began taking higher-level classes that built on the fundamentals I had previously learned. My renewed vigor to better understand processes in the human body so that I could one day help those in need enabled me to begin excelling in my classes. Taking classes that *intricately* taught me the foundation of physiological systems such as the endocrine, respiratory, and circulatory systems gave me a *euphoric* yearning to learn more. My *once frustrating* classes became fundamental steps to understanding and *reciprocally* appreciating the wonders of the human body.

Although the beauty and complexity of the human body inspires me to study science and participate in research, it is my passion to help those in need that drives me toward medicine. Although I have worked in underprivileged communities and have volunteered to assist others my entire life, as a physician I will have the tools to help those most in need. My ability to provide hope, care, and empathy to underprivileged communities will be my priority *and greatest glamor*. My compassion would allow me to sincerely relate with the patient, allowing us to work together toward successful treatment. My *instinctive* passion to help those in need has heightened my desire to be a physician.

As a physician, my *insatiable* thirst for knowing more about the extraordinarily complex human body would drive me to performing research and to help those in need. I expect to learn medicine by researching the human brain, the enigmatic organ that most intrigues me. With my background in psychology, I believe I can integrate my love of biological systems with my *intense* interest of the human brain. By better understanding the localized integrated functions of the human brain, I can further help recognize the causes of brain disorders and related phenomena. The importance of the human brain in controlling the physiological functions of the human body is unquestioned, and the knowledge of how it works is still very limited. I expect to research many of these unanswered questions and develop treatments to better the lifestyles of those with brain defects. This unyielding drive to unlock the remaining mysteries of the human body while helping better the lives of others will not only undoubtedly fulfill my role as a physician, but as a person as well.

APPENDIX C

HYPOTHETICAL WRITTEN RESPONSES TO SPECIFIC QUESTIONS FOR ADMISSION TO A MEDICAL SCHOOL IN A STUDENT'S SOPHOMORE YEAR OF COLLEGE

- What honors did you receive while in high school/college?

AP Scholar with Distinction Award
Illinois State Scholar
Prairie State Achievement Award for Math and Science
National Honor Society Member
Spanish Honor Society Member
Carl Sandburg High School Honor Roll (eight semesters)
St. Xavier University Dean's List
Sheriff's Youth Service Medal of Honor
President's Volunteer Service Award
Mid-Suburban League All-Academic Senior Athlete Award
Carl Sandburg High School Athletic Wall of Fame (four years)
Sportsmanship Award from Chicago District Tennis Association (2007)
Ranked #1 in Doubles in Chicago District Tennis Association (2008)

- In what extracurricular, community, and/or vocational activities have you participated while in high school/college?

High School Varsity Tennis Team (Second Doubles each year, State Qualifier each year. My team finished sixth in state my freshman and sophomore years, and finished fourth in state my junior and senior years.)
High School Student Ambassador (2008)
Volunteer at St. Alexius Medical Center (2006-2010)
St. Xavier University Tennis Team (#1 singles and #1 doubles)
St. Xavier University Pre-Health Club (Public Relations Co-Chairman)
St. Xavier University Habitat for Humanity
St. Xavier University Intramural Basketball
Kappa Kappa Gamma (Recording and Corresponding Secretary)

- If you have been employed during the regular school year while in high school/ college, specify type of work and approximate hours per week, currently and previous to this year.

During my sophomore year of high school, I worked for the Park District as both a lifeguard and a swim instructor for approximately ten hours per week. Throughout my junior and senior years of high school, I worked as a transporter for the Radiology Department at St. Alexius Medical Center for approximately sixteen hours per week. As a transporter, I brought the inpatients from their rooms down to the Radiology Department where they would get X-rays, an MRI, a CT scan, an ultrasound, etc. In addition to my position as a transporter, while I was a senior in high school, I worked as a medical assistant for Northwest Health care for four hours each week. In this position, I prepared patients for the physician. I would bring a patient to a room, take his or her vitals, and discuss with the patient the reason for his or her visit and the medications he or she was currently taking. I would then record this information in the patient's chart for the physician to reference.

- How have you spent your summers during high school?

During the summer of 2006, I volunteered in Piura, Peru. My volunteer work consisted of housing construction, food and clothing delivery, teaching English to children, as well as volunteering at an orphanage. During the summer of 2007, I attended health class in summer school. During the summer of 2008, I worked full-time as a lifeguard and swim instructor. I also did volunteer work in Costa Rica with Rustic Pathways. Rustic Pathways is a youth volunteer program that offers high school students the opportunity to travel to one of many different countries and partake in community service projects. During my volunteer time in Costa Rica, I did construction work for environmental projects. I painted and constructed fences for a local elementary school, as well as taught English to children and families. I also built hatcheries and participated in night walks to protect turtle eggs from predators.

During the summer of 2009, I worked approximately forty hours per week at St. Alexius Medical Center as a transporter for the Radiology Department. During the summer of 2010, I had an unpaid internship at the University of Illinois, College of Pharmacy, which was designed to introduce students to the field of clinical research.

I shadowed a physician while she saw patients in an epilepsy clinic, aided in editing a textbook, and attended Toxicon. (Toxicon is a consortium of medical students, residents, and fellows from emergency departments and pediatrics. At the Toxicon meetings, we discussed the cases of patients who entered Illinois hospitals due to toxic ingestions.) I also took part in a journal club, and learned about the grant application process, IRB (institutional review board), and OPRS (office for the protection of research subjects). I also worked about sixteen hours per week as a transporter. There was also a two-week period during that summer when I traveled to Seville, Spain, with a group of students from my high school. While in Spain, I attended class every day to learn about the language and the culture. We also went on tours around the city and learned about the history of many historical sites. In addition, every summer throughout high school, I volunteered at St. Alexius Medical Center for four hours each week. Also, I played tennis two hours per day, at least five days per week each summer.

- What do you feel is your greatest academic strength? Explain.

I think my greatest academic strength is that I tend to grasp new material quickly, especially math and science classes, because I am good at conceptualizing. This year during winter term, I took calculus; every day I needed to use my problem solving skills. For example, I was trying to find the distance between a point and a plane in three-dimensional space. It is easy for me to picture this and realize that I need to solve this problem by finding the vector that both contains the given point and is perpendicular to the plane. I am able to analyze the big picture, figure out what I need to do, and use what I have been taught to solve the problem. I am capable of looking through a chapter and grasping the concepts in one night. However, knowing the concepts only allows me to begin the problem. Time and experience have taught me that grasping concepts quickly puts me in between not having any information and having enough knowledge to be able to solve the problems.

Even though I understand the problems and how to begin them, I do need to put forth time and effort solving many practice problems to thoroughly master new material. I have come to realize that once I figure out how to address one type of problem, my curiosity intrigues me to learn the next concept, meaning I take pleasure in the pursuit of more information. Also, due to the fact that I have been more inclined in the sciences, I decided to go against what is considered the normal track of my high school. Ordinarily, students would take biology as freshmen, honors chemistry as sophomores, honors physics as juniors, then AP Biology, AP Chemistry, or AP Physics as seniors. However, I decided to challenge myself by skipping honors physics in order to take AP Biology as a junior and AP Physics as a senior. I felt that this switch would be important in order to best prepare myself for college and to challenge myself academically.

- What do you feel is your greatest non-academic strength? Explain.

I feel my greatest non-academic strength is that I am morally and ethically strong. I grew up in a home where two different religions are observed and while this could have been confusing for me, I found it to be extremely educational. I was able to see how the two religions are practiced and how, even though there were differences, both of the religions were based on truth, honesty, and kindness. It has been instilled in me to treat individuals with kindness, and I have been raised with the moral code of treating others the way that I would want to be treated. Today, I find that I am interested in people's differences, probably because of the way I was raised.

- What do you feel is your greatest academic weakness? Explain.

While I love to read, my greatest academic weakness is my reading speed. When I read, I sub-vocalize, to use the term that was taught to me. This means that I say each word in my mind while reading, thus slowing me down and making reading a sometimes frustrating task. To change this habit, during this upcoming term, I am taking an independent study with the director of St. Xavier University's Center for Teaching and Learning. The director is the person who taught me about sub-vocalizing, and he has worked with many students to improve their reading. During this course, I will learn to increase my reading speed as well as to improve my comprehension. I recognize that medical school requires a tremendous amount of reading, and I believe this course will prove to be very useful to me.

- What do you feel is your greatest non-academic weakness? Explain.

I tend to be a little cautious when I first meet people. I want to avoid saying things that might cause people to misread me, which leads me to being less talkative than I might be when I encounter a new acquaintance. Although I become much more self-aware and careful with what I say, I also become more observant with my listening skills when I am in these situations. My cautiousness allows me to avoid jumping to assumptions but it can inhibit spontaneous interaction. I like to think that my being cautious explains why I work well with teams or groups. Because there is less focus on me, I can contribute without the pressure of leading the group. I am confident that I will improve on this weakness with time and practice, and with the confidence that comes by taking my medical training seriously. I have already attempted to improve this weakness by choosing a job that was outside my comfort zone. In this position, in order to comfort others, I was forced to be more outgoing with fellow employees and patients; it certainly increased my self-confidence in starting conversations with people I do not know.

- Who do you feel will be most likely to provide you emotional support while in college and medical school? Give relationship and reason for choosing this person(s).

My mother and my father will provide me with support throughout undergraduate school and medical school. They have always been there to support me in everything that I have wanted to accomplish. They taught me the morals and values that I live my life by. Because of them, I work hard and respect, help, and care about others. Due to the fact that they both attended college in the medical field, they will be able to help me adjust to the differences between medical school and undergraduate school; they will provide me with support through their experiences.

- List your hobbies in order of importance to you.

My hobbies include tennis, snow skiing, snowboarding, playing chess, reading, water skiing, and playing leisure sports such as basketball, volleyball, and golf. I enjoy physically demanding activities that allow me to relieve stress and unwind from mentally strenuous activities during school.

- State one major problem you encountered during the last three years and explain how you dealt with it.

I have been extremely fortunate throughout my life in that I have not encountered very many large problems. However, I was challenged during my first trimester of college when I had to deal with the passing of my grandfather. It was my first time living away from home and I found it to be very difficult to deal with my loss especially because I was far away from my family. Although I was able to go home for a few days to grieve with my family, the pain had not subsided upon my return to St. Xavier University. I recognized that this was not a problem that I could resolve on my own, so I took it upon myself to use the resources available at St. Xavier such as counselors, friends, and my RA in order to find support during such a hard time. Witnessing my father's pain made me realize that the most important thing for me to do at that time was to be there for him. Upon my return to school, I called him every day to let him know that he was not alone through this tragedy. This situation was particularly difficult because it occurred a week before finals. I had to reorganize myself and use my time management skills in order to give myself time to grieve, time to call my family, as well as time to study for finals.

- How do you feel that Michigan State Medical School can contribute to your growth and development as a professional in the field of medicine?

Because Michigan State is a very close community, I feel that I will be encouraged to learn the sciences and skills that are necessary for a physician. I also will be taught how to apply my integrity for the patient's benefit. Michigan State offers individual attention from faculty. I have had the opportunity to speak to several physicians regarding the medical schools they attended. Some have referred to their experiences as "assembly line" training where they were just a "number or a statistic" in their medical class. This is not the medical education experience that I am interested in. Several Michigan State students, including my brother, stated that this was not their experience. They tell me that they have been given an outstanding individual education. They learned from teachers and preceptors who treated them with respect and who did not patronize them; their instructors were available and approachable. My brother felt his training at Michigan State led him to score extremely high on his Step 1 exam and led him to receive the AOA award. I am confident that Michigan State Medical School will provide me with a quality medical education.

Michigan State University Medical Center has an outstanding reputation. As you know, in the 2010 *US News* and *World Report*'s issue on "America's Best Hospitals," Michigan State was ranked in the top fifty in several specialties. It has recently opened a new orthopedic building where the physicians have become nationally known for their minimally invasive orthopedic surgeries. The new outpatient Cancer Center has become an example for combining patient comforts with state-of-the-art medical technology. The new Michigan State Hospital is scheduled to open in 2012 and is going to be a leader in the newest advances in medical care. I would feel honored to be a part of this growing medical network.

I will be able to gain the ability to fulfill a physician's responsibility to a patient with competence and compassion. Sustainability at Michigan State is something that is very important to me. Because Michigan State is known as being well-rounded in all specialties, I will be able to explore all of my options in order to choose what specialty I would like to pursue. I will also have the opportunity to experience a wide variety of specialties during my third year and fourth year rotations in order to learn what field of medicine I want to pursue. Michigan State's hospital network will give me the opportunities a medical student needs to grow and develop.

I plan on continuing to be involved in community service while I attend medical school. The Michigan State Community Service Initiative Program (MSCSIP) that is offered will allow me to continue performing community service. For example, I would like to be involved with the Buddies Program. I would love to have the opportunity to mentor a chronically ill child, which would be a very rewarding experience for me. Another community service program that Michigan State offers that particularly interests me is the MammoVan Program, through which I can help educate an underserved population about women's health issues. Due to a combination of all of the above, I feel Michigan State Medical School will provide me with the education, support, and growth needed in the field of medicine.

- Briefly describe your personal characteristics, which make you effective in working with people and outline your skills, interests, aptitude and temperament in relation to your suitability for a career in medicine.

Honesty, hopefulness, patience, empathy, and hard work are a few of my characteristics that make me effective in working with people. My honesty will help me deal with individuals facing illness. Patients value honesty in healthcare providers. My parents have always instilled in me the importance of being honest and this characteristic will support the interaction I will have with others. I like to think that I am not only honest with others, but also honest with myself. I understand that I, like everyone else, have room for improvement; I could be more self-confident and more knowledgeable about things like politics and world issues. I know that medical school will be tough and require a tremendous amount of time and effort. There will be many challenges that I will need to overcome, but I am prepared to face these challenges.

In being honest, it is important to balance that with hope. I am confident that as I gain more experience in caring for patients, I can provide a balance of hope and honesty about their disease.

I have tremendous patience. Being the youngest in my family with three older brothers has given me the ability to live through stressful situations and still remain patient. I have always shown empathy for others. During my volunteer experience in Peru, I felt the daily struggles of the people both medically and financially. It was during this time that reinforced my desire to become a physician and someday return to Peru to provide medical care.

I am hard-working. Whether it be in academics, employment, or athletics I have always put 100 percent into whatever I endeavor. For example, my senior year of high school I took AP Physics, which is normally taken after honors physics. Even though I had taken no prior physics class, I was confident that I could succeed in this course because I was willing to put in the extra effort that was required in order to receive a better education. I feel all of these qualities will benefit me as I pursue a career in medicine.

- What other career possibilities have you considered and why have you rejected them?

Because I enjoy science and math, I looked at possibilities within these two areas. Taking into account that I want a career that is mentally stimulating and personally rewarding, the two choices that I was most seriously considering were engineer and physician. However, I believe that a career as a physician would be much more personally rewarding because I would have the privilege to help and to make a difference in the lives of others on an almost daily basis.

- Briefly describe your experiences in working with people, the general responsibilities of each, and how long you held the position. If you have had limited experiences in working with people in the health field, be sure to list any life experiences, both paid or voluntary, include high school, college, or community service.

For the four years that I volunteered at the hospital, I had the responsibilities of completing the discharge of patients and escorting outpatients to the Radiology Department. Although the likelihood of a problem occurring was fairly small, we were still required to know how to handle a situation if a problem occurred. For example, I escorted a patient who was extremely combative to the point where I needed to ask for a code to be called. When I called the code, security arrived quickly and helped me take the patient back to his room where we were able to calm him down. In that small moment, I was responsible for the patient's safety and for the safety of everyone around him. It wasn't until later that I realized that we are all called upon to serve in such capacities, large and small. During my sophomore year and the following summer,

I worked as a lifeguard and a swim instructor. I worked with other lifeguards, club members, and children taking swim lessons. I was responsible for the safety of everyone in and around the pool and was trained in CPR and first aid. Eventually, I left this position in order to pursue my job as a hospital transporter.

As transporter, I learned how to handle different situations: projectile vomiting, incontinence, cardiac arrest, uncomfortable patients, and overly involved family members, to name a few. I maintained this position while also working as a medical assistant at a physician's office during my senior year. I had the responsibility of bringing patients to the examining room and preparing them for the physician. For this position, I was trained in taking vitals, performing finger stick glucose tests, and performing urinalyses. I had to recognize if the patients needed tests to be performed in office before the physician met with them. For example, if the patient was suffering from back pain and had no explanation for that pain, then I recognized that I should perform a urinalysis before the physician met with the patient.

- What plans do you have following graduation from medical school?

At this point in time, I am unsure of which field of medicine I plan on pursuing. I do want to go into a field that emphasizes the patient/physician relationship because I love working with people, and I have loved interacting with many patients while volunteering and working at a hospital. I would like to practice in the Chicagoland area. However, while I was doing volunteer work in Piura, Peru, there was a nurse who would attend to the ill, and physicians would only come about once a month from the larger cities nearby. After witnessing this lack of good health care, I would like to spend some time, perhaps several weeks each year, practicing in an impoverished area of the world similar to Piura. Overall, I am staying open-minded and am excited to explore many different options that the study of medicine offers.

- _For Personal Comments._ [Use this space or attach a sheet explaining the basis for your decision to become a physician and also to describe how your receiving an early Michigan State admission commitment would affect your undergraduate program.]

My decision to become a physician has been a progressive process. At a young age, I had been most interested in science class. This interest developed as I became more and more curious about the science behind everything, whether it is how molecules interact or how the human body works. Due to the fact that medicine and medical practice are always evolving, I think being a physician will give me the privilege to continuously learn new things. It will be intellectually demanding every day, which is something I look for in a profession.

Upon entering high school, I decided that volunteering at a hospital would help me to decide whether or not being a physician would be a career that I would want to pursue. Being exposed to different aspects of health care only sparked my interest further. I then decided to apply for a position as a transporter for the Radiology Department. My interaction with numerous patients with a wide variety of different diagnoses made me determined to pursue a job within the medical field.

My participation in the internship at the University of Illinois, College of Pharmacy, has sparked my interest in research. I am hoping that an early admission to Michigan State Medical School will allow me to be involved in an extended research project and, perhaps, to study abroad, maybe in Denmark, where they practice socialized medicine.

Volunteer work and helping others is very important to me. It has always been something that I thoroughly enjoy. I first realized how rewarding it is to assist others when I went to Piura, Peru, and had the opportunity to make a difference in the lives of those living without running water in homes made of burlap sacks. Ever since that experience, I have continued to volunteer. I volunteered at a hospital every week. I did construction work in Costa Rica. I became a member of Habitat for Humanity. I also organize bingo at a nursing home every Christmas Eve. My compassion and desire to help others results in my volunteer work. Being a physician will allow me to help others in the most intimate of ways, how they experience themselves and their health.

If I were to have the advantage of an early Michigan State admission commitment, it would allow for me to experience the fullness of the St. Xavier curriculum, conduct research, and perhaps even travel abroad.

Comment: *This student did an excellent job of responding to all questions.*

APPENDIX D

ONE STUDENT'S PREPARATION FOR MEDICAL SCHOOL

1. Describe a valuable experience in your personal development. This might be a decision you have made, an achievement of which you are particularly proud of, or a person who has influenced your life.

I am a poor-to-middling public speaker. I'm not nervous; I'm just not good at it. However, around last January, the National Collegiate EMS Foundation put out an advertisement for a competition in which a collegiate EMT would give an hour-long academic lecture on a topic relevant to collegiate EMS. I am a member of MIT EMS, and at the time I had recently run a call alongside a city ambulance. I was struck by the fact that my service had to, and did, provide the same level of care to our patients as the city's service, while being exposed to a significantly lower variety of calls. I decided to make a presentation based on how our service coped with the challenge where our most experienced EMT had all of three and a half years of time treating patients, and the best practices that we had adapted as a result. I prepared a proposal, requested feedback and edits from my fellow EMTs, and sent it in. I ended up being picked as a finalist, one of six chosen to give a talk at the conference that would count for continuing education credit. Realizing that I needed to rehearse if I was to have any chance at being successful, I sent out a request to my service for volunteers to evaluate a dress rehearsal. Around ten of my fellow EMTs showed up, and their feedback was brutal. My slides were poorly designed, concepts were explained poorly, and my speech was too rapid. I made some changes, and a week later, invited them to a second rehearsal. Once again, deficiencies were pointed out: my posture was poor, hand gestures were odd, verbal tics were obvious. But, I was told that I had at least gotten better While it was hardly perfect, I'm proud of the effort I put in and the final result.

2. Provide in detail an experience of working with individual(s) from diverse background(s). What was the experience? How did it have an impact on you?

I grew up in a suburban bubble, and my friends' parents were almost exclusively college-educated professionals. Before I came to college, I had never seen anyone underage drink alcohol or smoke a cigarette, let alone use illegal drugs. In my mind, drug use was something criminals and "other" people did, and a person who smoked was automatically worthy of contempt for their idiocy. Then I came to college. Most others shared my view on cigarette and drug use but a minority did not, and many of my fellow students in my dorm regularly smoked cigarettes and used marijuana. Initially, I held them all in contempt, and avoided studying or working on homework together with them. Then I slowly realized that when they weren't smoking or drinking, they were actually fine people. My impression slowly started to change. One night, I finally asked one avid smoker named Nate why he didn't quit, and his answer was astonishingly simple: It was his choice. He knew the risks, and even had a grandparent with COPD. But, it was how he'd been raised. He was set on joining the Marines, figured "he wouldn't live forever anyway," and decided that this would be his vice, just as it had been his father's. I argued ferociously with him, but finally came to accept his choice. Much else about him was foreign to me: While we worked on homework, he'd frequently take small breaks every hour or so to randomly play videogames or otherwise have fun, before getting back on task. As an eighteen-year-old freshman, he'd frequently get smashed. And of course, his style of speaking was distinctly slow, Southern, and backwater. But, I rapidly appreciated his intelligence and outlook. By sophomore year, we were helping each other pass test after test, and have become great friends. Since then I've been exposed to hundreds of smokers and alcohol abusers through my work in primary care and in EMS, and my contempt has changed to something closer to understanding. Still, meeting and working with Nate was critical to my change in attitude toward a great swath of people I would have previously dismissed out of hand.

3. **What do you hope to contribute to the field of medicine? And what do you hope to get out of a career in medicine?**

I would like to become an academic physician, carrying out research in healthcare organization, healthcare delivery, or medical devices, in addition to an active clinical practice. Further on in my career, I would hope to take more of a leadership role in managing a hospital or working in the Public Health Service or similar organization. As an engineer, my job and predilection is to fix things, whether they be machines, organizations, or people's bodies. I would like to contribute to the field of medicine by helping to improve all of the above: developing better medical devices, establishing organizations that deliver better care, and directly taking care of patients.

In terms of what I hope to get out of medicine, I am still inspired by figures such as Dr. W., Dr. E., and Dr. K. All three are over one hundred years old, still seeing patients, and claim they'll never retire. All of them have the same advice: love what you do. I see medicine as a field that I can love. Work will hopefully never feel like work, because every day I'll be looking forward to doing what I do. In medicine, there are opportunities to exercise leadership and to work on one's own; to creatively think up new solutions and to apply learned skills with discipline and precision; to be caring and compassionate but also to display calm and dispassion under pressure. In short, medicine offers a chance for a varied and fulfilling professional life, one that I hope I will never tire of.

Northwestern I cannot express how much I am looking forward to Northwestern's PBL curriculum, and how well it will fit my learning style. My personality's fit for Northwestern comes through best in my performance in a class called Microcomputer Project Lab. When

I started, I had the barest conception of what a microcontroller was – I only knew from the rumor mill that the class was hard, but rewarding and that it fulfilled a requirement. The professor didn't really teach us all that much. Instead, he provided us with chips, wire, and electromechanical equipment, and assigned large but clearly defined tasks. The only way we learned was to read technical manuals, and figure out on our own how to put it all together. I ended up building a very rudimentary X-ray-like sensor, a telephone dialer, and various other devices from scratch. I loved it, both for the knowledge and the collegial atmosphere. Many of my fellow students and I regularly worked till the lab closed at 11:45 p.m. figuring out how to design and build the devices. We'd curse, commiserate, order pizza, and help each other fix whatever wasn't working. By the end of the class, I had to come up with an independent final project. My grade was set, but I decided I wanted to end with a bang. I researched ACLS protocols, learned a few aluminum machining techniques, and refreshed my knowledge of kinematics. The result was a rudimentary ACLS simulator, with a physical "beating heart." This experience is just one example of how I much prefer classes that allow me to learn on my own.

More generally, I am constantly seeking knowledge on my own. I used to read the newspaper cover to cover, and now peruse CNN instead. I've even tried to improve my skills as an EMT-Basic outside of any formal curriculum. I've learned from several YouTube lectures created for the Northwestern University Rotating Resident Curriculum; and audited an ATLS course at the Boston Medical Center. I also love to teach and pass on this knowledge to my fellow EMTs. Finally, if it isn't evident in all of the above, let me say it again – I cannot describe how excited and prepared I am for Northwestern's curriculum.

I use a wide variety of coping strategies to deal with stressful situations, and I feel in general that I am well prepared for the stress of medical school. I cannot express how much I am looking forward to Northwestern's PBL curriculum, and how well it will fit my learning style. But I think my personal characteristics and how they'll help me at Feinberg will be evident in a story.

When I first joined MIT EMS, I found that many of the older EMTs subscribed to an old philosophy on training rookies: mistakes should be instantly and severely criticized. This was my first real exposure to such vicious criticism, and initially my confidence was severely shaken. On one call, I couldn't take a patient's blood pressure while we bounced along in the back of an ambulance with the sirens screaming en route to the hospital. The resulting dressing down after dropping off the patient lasted ten minutes, took place in front of my peers, and was utterly humiliating. However, I endured, and soon began to rationalize the criticism: at least I was told exactly what I was doing wrong. It was a direct feedback loop: the harsher the criticism, the faster I would improve. And so I did – my confidence recovered with my new perspective, and my skills rapidly progressed. Now, I am the one responsible for teaching new EMTs. While

I don't subscribe at all to the yelling and humiliation that I was subjected to, I still directly tell my juniors exactly what they are doing wrong.

Also, while I hate to rely on others, I have come to recognize that friends and colleagues are an invaluable resource. When I first started MIT, and was faced with a confluence of several tests and projects, I would try to "tough it out." Projects in which I was working with a team would take priority, followed by the subjects I was weakest in. All my activities would continue as normal. I distinctly recall leading my fraternity brothers in bailing out our flooded kitchen for two hours when I had an economics exam and major statistics project due the next day. However, as I was loaded with heavier responsibilities and harder courses, I slowly began to rely on my friends when I truly needed to. I found my fellow EMTs were more than happy to cover my shifts, as I would do when they faced crunch times. My fraternity brothers gladly helped me study for an exam in a class they had taken last year. My academics in general became a little easier once I learned to ask for help when I needed it.

My summer job in a solo primary care practice was probably the single largest impulse for me to become a doctor. I was exposed to the "front lines" of medicine in a way I had never previously been – my work as an EMT on a college campus didn't compare at all. I also had a terrific mentor in Dr. B., whom I worked for. I met an incredible variety of people, all with fascinating and saddening stories: a father and owner of a small business too embarrassed to tell his children he was incontinent due to rectal cancer; a thirty-year veteran teacher with hypertension, hypercholesterolemia, and diabetes in total denial that she needed any medication; a lonely eighty-year-old with no one left after his wife, who was also our patient, passed away. I couldn't imagine how they all mustered the strength to get through the day. I would frequently get to them first to take vitals and a history, and they'd perk up a bit, glad to finally be seen. But they lit up when Dr. B. walked in. She would greet each and every one with a smile, ask about their lives, and then proceed to put to rest their concerns. She would rapidly diagnose any new problems and had a literal encyclopedia of tests, drugs, and dosages in her head; and knew which ones were covered by which insurance to boot. Even when she could do nothing but talk, she would. I saw her spend an hour with a lonely, elderly woman whose husband had just died trying to convince her to go to therapy. She eventually did, and came back a month and a half later with her face and hair all made up – I almost didn't recognize her. Our patients struggled with pain or depression, and were seen an hour late or more, but almost all left feeling a little happier and a little better after Dr. B. talked with them. Throughout the summer, I saw first-hand the incredible power to do good a doctor wields. Even the patients with debilitating diseases that we could do little for – paraplegics, a poorly compliant schizophrenic, and others – left her office smiling and saying "thank you." The experience revealed how much good I could do if I dedicated my life to the practice of medicine, and how rewarding it could be.

Stanford The Stanford curriculum's scholarly concentration will help me develop my background in engineering and use it to find solutions to healthcare problems. I have heard from several current residents that during medical school, they became focused on exams and grades, and lost sight of what they'd hoped to do when they first entered medical school. However, with Stanford's requirement of a scholarly concentration, there is a clear path and stimulus to stay focused on my goals. In particular, the bioengineering, health services and policy research, and medical education foundation areas all align with my interests, and the global health application area is also appealing. These areas can all serve as conduits through which I can gain experience in applying my engineering skills to medicine.

While an Indian-American male from an upper middle class background is hardly a rare sight on a medical school campus, the perspective I bring as an engineer sets me apart. In particular, as an aerospace engineer, I have had training in large team organization and human-machine interaction. In terms of the former, my department's capstone course throws its entire graduating class to work on a real-world project to design and build a satellite or small air vehicle from scratch, forcing a group of thirty-ish people to organize and function like a company. In terms of the latter, MIT's curriculum emphasizes making machines easy and intuitive to use. For example, in my aerospace biomedical class, it was pointed out that a spacesuit that doesn't remind a spacewalking astronaut which button increases the air-conditioning and which shuts off the oxygen supply will lead to very unhappy (and very dead) astronauts. This is a non-trivial problem when all these buttons are mounted on the suit's torso, and the astronaut can't look down because the helmet is rigidly attached to said torso. The same principle is relevant to the design of anesthesia machines, where it should be very hard to turn the flow of oxygen down to zero, and very easy to tell what button does what. These experiences will allow me to evaluate and conduct research on medical organizations and medical machine user-interfaces, as well as bring a different mind-set to a variety of problems. I have also clocked over one thousand hours as an EMT. As I worked in a collegiate EMS organization, where in two years one becomes one of the most senior members, my duties now include teaching the new EMTs. Thus, I have had the heavy responsibility of teaching others skills that they must know to properly care for other people's lives. This burden has given me a new insight into what my instructors did to train me, and will serve me well in medical school, residency, and beyond.

Georgetown Why Georgetown and what will it do for my career? First, I was pleasantly surprised to learn from the website that Georgetown has made the ownership of a hand-held Smartphone mandatory, and has integrated it into the curriculum. As an engineer, I know very well that the use of software in critical tasks has made many services safer and more efficient. Even the great piloting of Captain Chesley Sullenberger, who glided his plane into the Hudson River, was helped by the plane's software-based controls, which let him fly without worrying that his aircraft was about to fall out of the sky. Similarly, computer-based tools can frequently help deliver medical care with fewer errors and greater speed, and Georgetown clearly recognizes this with its curriculum. I hope to benefit, learn from, and contribute to such an environment, one that clearly encourages the use of the latest technology to improve medical education and the delivery of care.

Secondly, I am looking forward to a curriculum that formally covers the intangibles of a career in medicine. Even as an EMT on a college service, I have seen fellow students "sucked in" to working on the ambulance, with both their grades and eventually their patient care compromised as a result. Others became extremely technically competent, but never displayed much empathy to their patients. (Though MIT EMS tries to weed out those who became EMTs for the adrenaline rush of driving with lights and sirens screaming, we are about as successful at it as medicine has been at controlling costs.) The seventeen objectives/desired competencies of Georgetown are a good way to stay focused on the fact that being a doctor takes more than the simple memorization of factoids regarding the human body. This will be invaluable throughout medical school and during my actual career, when the intangibles will come fully into play.

Thirdly, I find Georgetown's location quite attractive. Being in Washington, DC, is an incredible advantage. Health care's future in America will literally be decided less than an hour away from campus. It may be naive to hope that a medical school student can contribute to a process hijacked by several hundred million dollars' worth of lobbying. Nevertheless, the experience should still prove invaluable to my understanding of where my profession will go in the future.

Finally, Georgetown's emphasis on service resonates strongly with me. The community service requirement provides a conduit to accomplish something I hoped to do in medical school regardless: use my skills and knowledge as I develop them to help those who are not nearly as fortunate as me.

Thank you for considering me for the Georgetown School of Medicine Class of 2016.

Columbia One strong appeal of P&S is the School of Engineering and Applied Sciences at Columbia University. My current research into designing an orthotic to correct drop foot and other neurological disorders is at the intersection of medicine and engineering, and I look forward to working with the world-class engineers at SEAS on interdisciplinary projects and research while in medical school. Another appeal is Columbia's location: an urban area with a diverse patient population. Indeed, I was very excited to hear about the CoSMO and CHHMP programs, through which I can make a positive impact and gain valuable clinical exposure to a variety of diseases. Finally, Columbia's P&S club and the strong student community it supports are quite attractive.

I would like to comment on two aspects of my application.

First, my engineering curriculum: My degree says aerospace engineering with information technology, but my exposure has been quite broad. In fact, up till junior year, I was on a track to double major in aerospace engineering and electrical engineering with computer science. I've taken courses in systems engineering, computation structures, software engineering, and microcontroller system design. The last course mentioned is a capstone engineering course for the Electrical Engineering/Computer Science Department. For my solo final project in that class, I researched basic cardiology, and then used my woodworking, machining, and coding skills to create a rudimentary ACLS simulator with a physically "beating" heart, powered by four motors. The system would simulate rhythms such as ventricular fibrillation and then respond to the correct intervention, as selected on a keypad, by going into normal sinus rhythm.

Secondly, my work as an EMT with MIT Emergency Medical Services included a large variety of opportunities. I audited an ATLS course at the Boston Medical Center as a patient, taught and mentored many junior EMTs, and attended the National Collegiate EMS Foundation's national conference. Before the conference, I applied for a speaking slot as part of a student speaker competition, and was selected as one of six finalists. I gave a lecture to around fifty other collegiate EMTs from around the nation, on how best to prepare and train for certain calls, such as cardiac arrests that are relatively rare on a college campus.

Currently, along with a graduate student supervisor, I have been researching orthotics for the correction of drop foot via the use of functional electrical stimulation. The technique we have been investigating is the use of surface electrodes located near the knee that stimulate the peroneal nerve, which innervates the tibialis anterior muscle. We then record the foot's resultant lift using inertial measurement units (IMUs) strapped onto the foot and shin. Over the course of my work, I have independently run subjects through trials; modified our experimental protocol; applied for a protocol modification from MIT's COUHES (Committee On the Use of Humans as Experimental Subjects); modified the Simulink software model we are using to control our stimulators; and, along with my supervisor, analyzed our data to develop a model that can predict the response of the tibialis anterior muscle to electrical stimulation across multiple subjects. We have just started to collect data, but we look forward to sending a paper for publication within the next year or so.

How I'd react to a situation where someone wasn't pulling their weight would depend a lot on the timeframe. If the time period is short and urgent, I'd just take up the slack myself. For example, I work on an ambulance service that typically runs three-person crews. When one of my teammates applied a splint that didn't stabilize the limb, or didn't perform a rapid and thorough interview, I'd immediately take over and do things properly. Afterwards, I'd go over what went wrong, and how that member of my team could do better. Similarly, if the group's deliverable was due the next day or so, I would do the extra work myself or jointly with another group member.

On the other hand, if the group had a longer deadline for its work, I'd take aside the group member and start a conversation. In my experience, few people are simply lazy or uncaring about a small group's objectives. Instead, they typically have other commitments or personal situations that prevent them from focusing on their work. Consequently, I'd offer to help them resolve their personal situation, or get the group to take some of the load off of their shoulders while they resolve their (hopefully) temporary predicament.

Yale There are literally one hundred reasons why I want to attend Yale for my medical education. But more important is what I can contribute to Yale's incredible environment and how Yale can help me achieve my career goals. I would like to become an academic physician, carrying out research in healthcare organization, healthcare delivery, or medical devices, in addition to an active clinical practice. Further on in my career, I would hope to take more of a leadership role in managing a hospital or working in the Public Health Service or similar organization.

Yale is a great place to start on the path to achieving all these aims. The interdisciplinary environment of the university is the perfect place to investigate medical devices and health care organizations. In terms of management, Yale's MBA program can provide me sound training for any leadership roles in the medical community. Finally, Yale's modern curriculum that emphasizes collaborative learning, patient contact, and clinical skills will provide an excellent background for any future clinician.

In terms of what I can bring to the table, my experiences are quite eclectic. As an aerospace engineering major, I have been trained to design and build must-not-fail human-mechanical systems. As a volunteer collegiate EMT I have taken care of a large variety of patients and have taken on a teaching role to my fellow EMTs. Finally, as a student leader, I am familiar with the challenges of running organizations. These backgrounds allow me to uniquely help the Yale School of Medicine achieve its goal of creating physician-leaders.

As an engineer, my job and predilection is to fix things, whether they be machines, organizations, or people's bodies. I would like to contribute to the field of medicine by helping to improve all of the above: developing better medical devices, establishing organizations that deliver better care, and directly taking care of patients. Yale is an extraordinary place that can prepare me to complete all three goals.

One more practice I've picked up that's worked well for me so far – after an interview and in some cases if I haven't heard from a school in a while, I send an activities update.

Dear Admissions Committee of the Columbia University College of Physicians and Surgeons,
Here is an update of my activities since submitting the AMCAS application in June.

1. Throughout the summer and for the beginning of the semester, I served as treasurer (one of the seven executive directors) of the MIT Career Fair. On September 21 I oversaw the largest and most profitable career fair in the history of the institute. To provide context, the previous year's fair saw approximately three hundred companies and brought in approximately $550,000 in revenue for MIT. This year's fair saw approximately three hundred fifty companies and brought in over $750,000 of revenue, while our expenses only increased by $40,000. (http://tech.mit.edu/V131/N39/career.html)

2. My research into functional electrical stimulation continues. After working full-time as a researcher throughout the summer, I have cut back to about six hours a week during this semester. I will likely publish a paper at the end of this semester or next, and I will be an author. I have proposed a new direction for the study: working with paraplegic patients at the Lahey Clinic in Burlington, MA, to acquire baseline data in the absence of conscious sensory response. I am currently seeking a neurologist to partner with at the clinic (several have expressed interest), and will submit a proposal to the IRB soon.

3. As I was working full-time over the summer, I took night classes at Harvard Summer School to fulfill my pre-medical requirements. I received an A- in Biochemistry w/Lab, and a B in Molecular Biology w/Lab.

4. I was selected as the MIT Undergraduate Association representative to the MIT Medical Consumers Advisory Commission for the 2011–2012 academic year. The Commission's role is to provide recommendations on how best MIT Medical can meet the needs of the community. At the first meeting, I introduced a proposal to study the rates of colds and general illnesses among students grouped by residence hall. If any dorms are hotspots of disease, it can be inferred that the dorm harbors particularly unhygienic conditions, and MIT Medical and Facilities can take steps to address the cause. The proposal was taken up for further consideration by the medical director.

5. As an EMT, I have been involved with many incidents involving student mental health issues. Consequently, after two undergraduate suicides in two months, I arranged a meeting on November 2, 2011, with the dean of student support services and MIT Medical's clinical director for campus life. I advocated changes to address several shortcomings of the current, relatively opaque system that discourages the reporting of other students' possible suicidal behavior to MIT Mental Health. The dean then took the shortcomings and suggestions to the chancellor, and discussion of possible improvements continues.

6. I also tried my hand at sailing in my nonexistent free time, and earned a sailing card at the MIT Sailing Pavilion.

Thank you again for your consideration of me for membership in your class of 2016. I am truly excited by the opportunities and curriculum at P&S.

———

Questions from my Columbia interview:

1. Before the interview itself, the dean of admissions sat all the applicants interviewing that day around a room, and went around asking about an "interesting thing" on our application. For me, it was my service as an EMT. He also asked us to tell everyone about an activity "that brings us bliss."
2. Interview was open file, and the interviewer had a few specific questions about my research and work as an EMT. Also, "Have you considered what specialty to pursue?", some public policy questions, and an extended discussion about various primary care issues, as the doctor was internal medicine.

———

I highly recommend for interviews that applicants familiarize themselves with medical specialties and current controversies/issues in the various fields. Having been interviewed by a primary care doctor at Columbia, when she asked about questions I had, I was able to ask, "So, what's your opinion on PSA testing/mammograms?" (When interviewed by an OB/GYN, I could instead bring up the C-Section vs. forceps vs. natural birth controversy. For a surgeon, I instead brought up palliative care and specialization/scope of practice issues.) My interviews have all gone exceptionally well once my interviewer realizes I know something about their specialty.

Two great books that I've found to be very good at covering current medical issues are *Complications* and *Better*, both by Atul Gawande. His blog is quite informative, too (his recent article about coaching in surgery and another about palliative care failures were both extraordinarily informative). I always tell my pre-med underclassmen friends to read them.

Comment: *Never mention the weather or activities – you're going to medical school, not selecting a vacation spot. This student did an excellent job of researching each school he was applying to*

RESOURCES

ABOUT.COM: THE NEW YORK TIMES NEWS SERVICE & SYNDICATE

"Many Students Have the Grades and the MCAT Scores – How Will You Stand Out?" by Andrea Santiago, About.com, December 12, 2011

ASSOCIATION OF AMERICAN MEDICAL COLLEGES

Average MCAT Scores and GPAs for Applicants and Matriculants: Applicant Matriculation File as of 10/19/2010

US Medical School First-Time Applicants, 2001–2011: AAMC Data Warehouse Applicant Matriculation File

US Medical School Total Applicants, 2001–2011: AAMC Data Warehouse Applicant Matriculation File

Applicants to US Medical Schools, 2004–2011: AAMC Data Warehouse Applicant Matriculation File

US Medical School First-Year Enrollment, 2001–2011: AAMC Data Warehouse Applicant Matriculation File

First-Year Enrollees to US Medical Schools, 2004 2011· AAMC Data Warehouse Applicant Matriculation File

US Medical School First-Time Applicants by Gender, 2001 2011: AAMC Data Warehouse Applicant Matriculation File

US Medical School First-Year Enrollees by Gender, 2001–2011: AAMC Data Warehouse Applicant Matriculation File

First-Year Enrollees and Total Applicants to US Medical Schools by Gender, 2011: AAMC Data Warehouse Applicant Matriculation File

US Medical School Applicants and Students 1982–1983 to 2010–2011Charts

Residency Applicants of US Medical Schools by Specialty and Sex, 2010

Getting into Medical School: *www.aamc.org*

Exploring a Medical Career· *www.aamc.org*

Creating a Study Plan: *www.aamc.org*

Candidates: *www.aamc.org*

The 2012 MCAT Essentials

The Road to Becoming a Doctor

Identifying Behaviors of Successful Medical Students and Residents: November 2001, Vol. 1, No.4

MODERN HEALTHCARE

"Medical School Applications Hit New Record, Enrollment up 3%, AAMC Finds," by Ashok Selvam, Modern Healthcare, October 24, 2011

"New Rounds for Med Students: Revised Admissions Test, Changing Focus for Essential Skills Will Bring a Fresh Look to the Next Generation of Physicians," by Andis Robeznieks, Modern Heathcare, February 27, 2012

YALE DAILY NEWS

"Future Pre-Meds will Take New MCAT" by Traci Tillman, Yale Daily News, April 6, 2011

ABOUT THE AUTHOR

EDWARD M. GOLDBERG

A native of Chicago's south side, Mr. Goldberg earned a Bachelor of Science in marketing from Northern Illinois University and a Master of Science degree in hospital and health service administration from The Ohio State University.

Mr. Goldberg has been a hospital administrator for thirty-eight years, initially being appointed as administrator of Coral Gables Hospital in Florida when he was twenty-three. From 1994 until his retirement in November of 2012, he served as the president/CEO of St. Alexius Medical Center, a 331-bed medical/surgical facility in Hoffman Estates, IL.

Mr. Goldberg has also previously served as a vice president for Columbia/HCA; administrator at Hargrove Hospital, Chicago IL; administrator at Charter Barclay Hospital, Chicago IL; and regional director with Charter Medical Corporation.

Under his leadership, each hospital Mr. Goldberg was responsible for had significant increases in admissions and outpatient visits. With a strong focus on physician, employee, and patient relations, he consistently achieved some of the nation's highest physician, employee, and patient satisfaction scores.

Although this is Mr. Goldberg's first book as an author, he has edited and published a book on cultural sensitivity and has provided numerous presentations to healthcare and other organizations on servant leadership, relationship development, and healthcare marketing.

Mr. Goldberg is now a hospital consultant, presenter, and coach for individuals applying to medical, dental, veterinary, residency, physician assistant, and nurse practitioner programs. He is available to review personal statements and help applicants develop their responses to interview questions, working with via telephone, via e-mail, and/or in person. For pricing and additional information regarding individual tutoring/coaching, please contact Mr. Goldberg at www.soyouwanttobeaphysician.com.

Mr. Goldberg is married to Linda Trytek and has two grown daughters, Katie and Erica, and a thirteen-year-old yellow lab named Zipper.

Made in the USA
Middletown, DE
17 November 2015